HOME REPAIR AND IMPROVEMENT

BATHROOM MAKEOVERS

OTHER PUBLICATIONS:

DO IT YOURSELF
Custom Woodworking
Golf Digest Total Golf
How to Fix It
The Time-Life Complete Gardener
The Art of Woodworking

COOKING
Weight Watchers® Smart Choice Recipe Collection
Great Taste~Low Fat
Williams-Sonoma Kitchen Library

HISTORY
Our American Century
World War II
What Life Was Like
The American Story
Voices of the Civil War
The American Indians
Lost Civilizations
Mysteries of the Unknown
Time Frame
The Civil War
Cultural Atlas

TIME-LIFE KIDS
Student Library
Library of First Questions and Answers
A Child's First Library of Learning
I Love Math
Nature Company Discoveries
Understanding Science & Nature

SCIENCE/NATURE
Voyage Through the Universe

For information on and a full description
of any of the Time-Life Books series listed above,
please call 1-800-621-7026 or write:

Reader Information
Time-Life Customer Service
P.O. Box C-32068
Richmond Virginia 23261-2068

HOME REPAIR AND IMPROVEMENT

BATHROOM MAKEOVERS

BY THE EDITORS OF TIME-LIFE BOOKS, ALEXANDRIA, VIRGINIA

The Consultants

Allan Ostroff is a plumber who has worked for more than 25 years building and renovating homes in the Montreal area.

Joe Teets is a master electrician/contractor. Currently in the Office of Adult and Community Education for the Fairfax County Public Schools, he has been involved in apprenticeship training as an instructor and coordinator since 1985.

Guy Tomberlin is a Virginia State Certified Master Plumber and contractor. He has been employed by Fairfax County, Virginia, since 1985, where he performed plumbing inspections for 12 years. Mr. Tomberlin also conducts plumber apprenticeship training as well as serving on multiple building code industry committees.

CONTENTS

The Powder Room

A few modest changes can make an ordinary half bath more appealing. Distinctive wall treatments can dress up a plain room, while a wall of mirror panels can make a small space seem larger. A set of matched plumbing fixtures, with a pedestal sink in place of a vanity, frees up floor area and unifies the decor. Special lighting and wall-to-wall carpeting can bring a cozy, luxurious feel to the bathroom.

Wallpapering around a toilet tank →

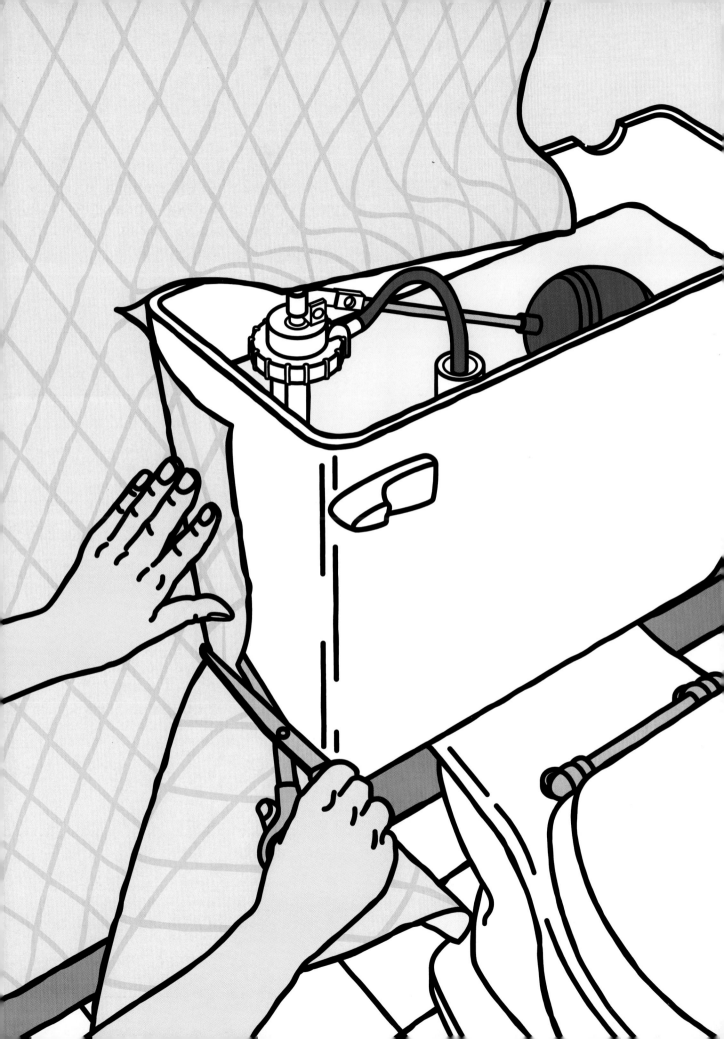

The Powder Room: A Place for Small Luxuries

Even a tiny powder room can be a showcase of your personal decorating tastes and style. Lack of space does not limit the makeover potential of a room; on the contrary, a small space is often easier to decorate than a large one—a clear case of less offering more.

Whatever your design preferences, adhering to a few simple rules of thumb will help ensure a successful outcome. When selecting colors, keep in mind that pale tones make a small room seem larger; however, you need not shun dark hues altogether. When thoughtfully chosen and applied, strong colors can create dramatic effects in an enclosed space that are often difficult to duplicate in larger rooms. Deep forest green or rich burgundy, for instance, may be just the right touch for a period-style bathroom or for achieving a sumptuous look in a modern one.

The toilet *(pages 32-35)* and sink *(pages 26-31)*, the obvious central features of a powder room, should match in color and

A wooden vanity and sponge-painted walls give this powder room an old-world charm. The pheasant pattern baked into the porcelain surfaces of the sink and toilet unifies the fixtures and blends with the style of the room.

The design of this faucet and countertop suits the unusual modern look of the basin, making the fixture a decorative element in itself. Space below the sink is put into use as storage, with a simple metal shelf that goes well with other components.

style, as well as make a contribution to the overall decorating scheme. For example, placing plumbing fixtures with a classic design against a backdrop of Victorian wallpaper and flowered carpeting can create a miniature world of nostalgia and romance. A set of streamlined fixtures with sleek faucets and fittings makes a bold, ultramodern statement when reflected in mirrored walls and glossy ceramic tiles.

The sink is a natural focal point in a half bath. Faucets and fittings are significant elements of the larger design, so treat them as parts of an ensemble and match their style to that of the sink, rather than selecting them on their individual merits. You can also

two of the most popular wall coverings for bathrooms, are manufactured in many styles, from traditional to post-modern. Or, combine these materials to create the look you want.

Mirrors are a necessity in a powder room, and they also provide an easy way to create the illusion of space. An entire wall of mirrors *(pages 20-22)* can double the apparent size of a room, while mirrored cabinets can become unobtrusive storage areas—a feature that is especially useful in a room equipped with a pedestal sink or a wall-hung sink, but no vanity.

Floor space, usually at a premium in a powder room, does not have to be sacrificed for storage. A simple, often overlooked solution is to go vertical—tall and narrow shelves or cabinets can actually make the room feel more spacious. Skirting below an open sink

expand a motif by coordinating other hardware in the room with the fixture fittings. Polished brass doorknobs and cabinet handles combined with brass sink faucets, for example, can add a touch of opulence; while porcelain fittings may recall earlier times. If the sink is set into a countertop, it should also harmonize with the style of the fixture. Ceramic tiles, natural stone, decorative laminates, and solid wood are some of the options from which to choose.

The choice for wall treatments is virtually limitless. Ordinary paint alone has nearly boundless decorative potential. Texturing, stenciling, and other special application techniques make it one of the most versatile materials of all *(pages 12-13)*. Ceramic tiles and wallpaper *(pages 14-15)*,

Low-profile toilets such as the one shown here are right at home in a small room. Their sleek, contoured design will complement almost any modern decor.

In this powder room, antique-style fixtures with scalloped bases and polished-brass fittings contrast sharply against the dark colors of the walls and floor. Bright light filtering in through large windows produces a dramatic effect.

can conceal baskets of toiletries or cleaning supplies from view.

Lighting is an important concern, especially in a bathroom without a window. One option is the cool illumination of overhead halogens. Or, you may want attractive incandescent wall fixtures in a style that matches other features in the room. You can also install bright lighting strips along the sides of the mirror to create a warm and complimentary glow *(pages 23-25).*

The finish flooring contributes greatly to the overall appearance of the space. Hardwood, tile, or stone can suit a range of tastes from elegant sophistication to rural practicality. Wall-to-wall carpeting *(pages 16-19)* brings instant warmth and the unmistakable sense of luxury to a small room.

Carefully chosen towels and bath accessories, in a style that complements the other elements in the room, help complete the picture. In general, however, avoid cluttering the space with nonessentials. You can bring a personal signature to the room with a few select items such as special soap holders, decorative towel racks, or framed pictures and wall hangings, but be prudent—too many objects may be overpowering.

Powder rooms can be dressed up creatively and inexpensively with paint applied in decorative patterns. By experimenting with the techniques on these pages, you can achieve a variety of effects. Whatever method you choose, practice first on a board or on a wall that can be easily repainted.

Choosing a Technique: Dragging a dry paintbrush through wet paint *(below)* forms a texture of vertical lines. Dabbing on paint with a sponge *(opposite)* creates a random design that appears to have depth. Scattered across the wall or applied as a neat border below the ceiling or above a baseboard or chair rail, stencils can be used to echo other elements in the room. If you want more than one color, purchase a set of stencils.

Washes and Glazes: The patterns illustrated on these pages are made with a wash or a glaze. Latex and acrylic products are easy to work with, and tools clean up effortlessly with water. Oil products are more durable than water-base paints; however, they take longer to dry and give off unpleasant and sometimes toxic fumes. Latex and acrylic can be applied only over flat paint; oil will adhere to gloss or semigloss paint, but you must sand the surface first to roughen it.

Washes and glazes are sold in a limited range of colors, but you can expand the selection by making your own: For latex paint, mix one part paint and two parts water. An acrylic glaze for sponging can be made from one part commercial acrylic glaze, two parts acrylic paint, and one part water; for dragging, change the proportions to five parts glaze, one part paint, and one part water. For an oil glaze, mix one part commercial oil glaze, one part alkyd paint, and one part paint thinner.

Preparing Walls: Before painting, repair cracks and holes, and sand high-luster paint to remove the gloss. Unless the existing paint is in good shape and you want to keep the color as a background, apply a base coat of flat latex or alkyd paint first. If the wall is papered, remove the wallpaper and sand the surface smooth.

⚠️ *Do not paint in a closed room—ventilate it by opening windows and doors. To prevent* **CAUTION** *spontaneous combustion of rags soaked in solvent, store them in sealed glass or metal containers.*

 TOOLS

Paintbrush or roller
Stiff-bristle paintbrush
Artist's paintbrush
Natural sponge
Synthetic sponge or
  stencil brush
Chalk line

 **MATERIALS**

Cloths
Glaze or wash
Paint
Stencils
Painter's tape

🪖 **SAFETY TIPS**

Wear goggles and rubber gloves when painting.

Dragging.
◆ With a paintbrush or roller, apply a vertical strip of glaze or wash about 18 inches wide to the wall.
◆ Press a dry, wide, stiff-bristle paintbrush at the top of the strip, then drag the brush down the wall.
◆ Wipe the brush clean with a dry cloth and drag it down the wall again, overlapping the previous stroke *(left)*.
◆ When you reach the edge of the strip, apply paint to the next one, and continue the process to texture the entire wall.

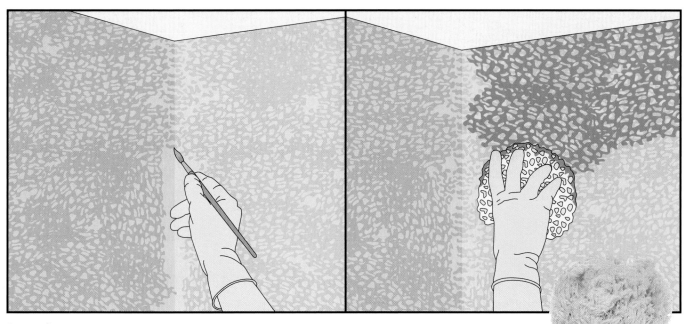

Sponging.

◆ For water-base paint, soak a natural sponge *(photograph)* in water, then wring it out. For oil-base paint, soak the sponge in the solvent recommended on the paint label, then squeeze out the excess and let it dry for one hour.

◆ Soak the sponge in the glaze or wash, then wring it until it stops dripping.

◆ Apply the sponge to the wall, twisting it slightly to create interesting patterns. Dab gently into corners to avoid applying too much paint.

◆ Replicate the sponge pattern in the corners with an artist's paintbrush *(above, left)*.

◆ Let the first coat dry. Then, if desired, follow the same technique to sponge a second color onto the wall *(above, right)*. Apply as many coats of color as you want.

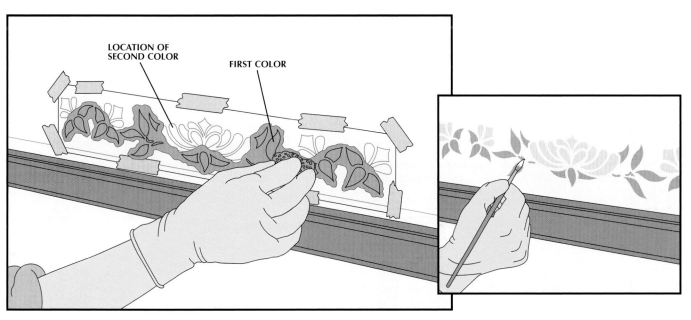

LOCATION OF
SECOND COLOR

FIRST COLOR

A stenciled border.

◆ With a chalk line, snap a level line on the wall to indicate the bottom of the row of stencils. Make a mark at the middle of the wall.

◆ Position the first stencil along the chalk line, centering it over the mark; fasten it in place with painter's tape.

◆ Dip a synthetic sponge or stencil brush in latex paint or artist's acrylic paint, then dab it on a piece of paper to remove excess paint. Dab the cut-out area of the stencil with the applicator *(above)*.

◆ Carefully remove the stencil and reposition it next to the painted area. Repeat the process as many times as necessary to complete the border. At a corner, bend the stencil or cut a duplicate to fit the remaining space.

◆ For a pattern with more than one color, allow the first color to dry, then apply the second color by aligning the second stencil to match the position of the first.

◆ Let the paint dry, then touch up the stenciled shapes using an artist's paintbrush dipped in the wall's original paint color *(inset)*.

Wallpapering

Wallpaper for a powder room or bathroom is applied in the same way as for any other room, but with a few special techniques to fit it around fixtures and pipes.

Choosing Paper: In a full bath, wallpaper must withstand very high humidity, but in a powder room, it is subjected to only an occasional splash of water. The chart below lists types of paper and a few important facts to consider when choosing paper for your project.

Preparing the Room: Before you begin papering, complete any new work on the walls, such as hanging mirror panels *(pages 20-22)*, then take down towel racks and other fixtures. Remove any old wallpaper and paste and wash the walls with a household cleaner, then apply a primer-sealer.

Hanging Wallpaper: For prepasted paper, cut a strip long enough to overlap the ceiling and floor by a couple of inches, then roll the piece and soak it in a water box. Align the strip over the ceiling line and press it down the wall with a smoothing brush. Trim off excess at the top and bottom. Butt successive strips edge to edge, matching the pattern. To paper around obstacles, use the methods shown opposite.

For unpasted paper, instead of soaking strips in water, lay them flat on a work surface and apply paste to their backs with a brush or paint roller.

 TOOLS

Scissors
Utility knife
Trimming guide
Water box
Paste brush
Smoothing brush

Wallpaper Choices for Powder Rooms and Bathrooms

Type of Paper	Advantages and Disadvantages
Cloth-backed vinyl	Relatively easy to hang, but somewhat difficult to fit around obstacles.
	Withstands high humidity.
	Not available prepasted.
	Easy to hang.
Paper-backed vinyl	Lighter weight than cloth-backed vinyl.
	Does not withstand high humidity.
	Available prepasted.
	Easy to hang.
Vinyl-coated paper	Looks more like paper than vinyl.
	Stains and tears more easily than vinyl.
	Does not withstand high humidity.
	Available prepasted.

Selecting the right paper.
Any of the three types of wallpaper listed at left can withstand the occasional splash that they will be subjected to in a powder room. Cloth-backed vinyl—also referred to as solid vinyl—is more difficult to hang than the others because it is not available prepasted and must be applied with a separate adhesive. For a room that is exposed to high humidity, however, cloth-backed vinyl is the best choice. For any bathroom, avoid delicate products such as foil and hand-screened papers.

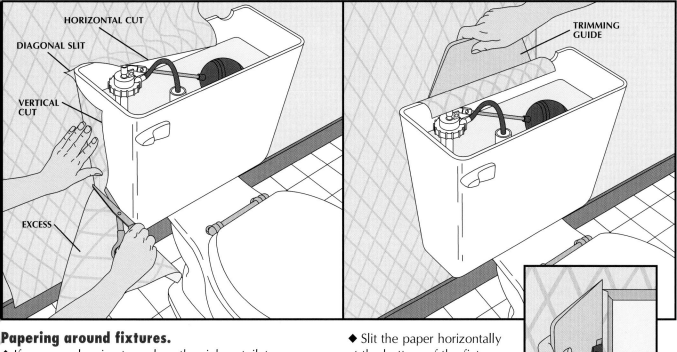

HORIZONTAL CUT

DIAGONAL SLIT

VERTICAL CUT

EXCESS

TRIMMING GUIDE

Papering around fixtures.

◆ If you are planning to replace the sink or toilet, remove them *(pages 27-28 and 32-33)* before you begin and paper the wall behind them. Otherwise, hang wallpaper up to within one strip of the fixture.

◆ Apply a sheet so it overlaps the ceiling by a couple of inches and align its pattern with the previous strip, letting the surplus at the bottom drape over the fixture.

◆ Press the paper against the wall above the fixture and, with scissors or a utility knife, cut the paper across the top of the fixture a few inches from the wall.

◆ Make a diagonal slit at the top corner of the obstacle.

◆ Press the paper against the wall beside the fixture, then cut vertically down the side, leaving a few inches of overlap, and stop an inch or two above the bottom of the fixture.

◆ Slit the paper horizontally at the bottom of the fixture *(above, left)* and trim off the excess.

◆ Smooth the paper against the wall; then, with a trimming guide or long ruler wrapped in a soft towel, wedge the paper beside, under, and up to the tank *(above, right)*.

◆ Follow the same procedure to fit any other wallpaper strips around the fixture.

In the case of a medicine cabinet or other object where you cannot wedge the paper behind it, use the same method but trim the paper to fit precisely around the edges of the obstacle *(inset)*.

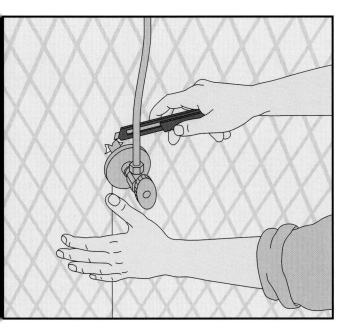

Fitting paper around pipes.

◆ Wallpaper up to within one strip of the pipe.

◆ Hang the next sheet, letting the bottom of it fall over the pipe.

◆ With a utility knife, make a vertical slit in the paper from the top of the pipe to the bottom of the strip.

◆ Push the slit paper against the wall, fitting it around the pipe.

◆ With a utility knife, cut neatly around the pipe where it enters the wall *(left)*.

Soft, warm carpeting is an affordable luxury for a powder room. Because of its exposure to moisture, as well as the need to clean it frequently, special bath carpet is the best choice; its synthetic pile and pliable latex backing allow for easy machine-washing. Held down with double-sided tape, it can be laid directly on the floor and removed for cleaning. Launder small carpets with mild soap and warm water in a regular washing machine, then tumble them dry at a low temperature. Wash large carpets in a commercial-size washing machine.

Buying Carpet: Bath carpet is generally available in 5- by 8-foot pieces and in rolls 6 or 8 feet wide. Measure the room's length and width and, if possible, buy carpet at least 6 inches larger in each dimension. If one piece will not fit, plan on laying down two or three sections.

Installation: Cut the carpet to the approximate size of the room, lay it down, then trim it to fit with a carpet knife. Orienting the carpet with the pile leaning toward the room's main door will give a full, rich appearance. In most cases, this requires simply placing the end of the roll at the entrance, but you can check the pile direction by stroking the carpet to see which direction raises the fibers.

The double-sided tape that secures the carpet is somewhat fragile; replace it whenever you remove the carpet for cleaning.

TOOLS

Carpet knife
Replacement blades
Metal yardstick
Cutting board

MATERIALS

Graph paper
Carpet
Double-sided carpet
   tape (2")

CUTTING AND LAYING

1. Drawing a diagram.
◆ Measure the floor space and make a scale drawing on graph paper of the bathroom, including fixtures and other obstructions. Label the wall adjacent to the longest uninterrupted wall—in this example, the one with the door—as the starting wall.
◆ Outline the carpet on the drawing, adding a 3 to 4-inch trimming allowance along all the edges except the starting wall *(right)*.
◆ Cut the carpet outline, turn it over, and mark the starting wall on its back. If you need more than one piece of carpet to fill the space, include the seam lines in the drawing.

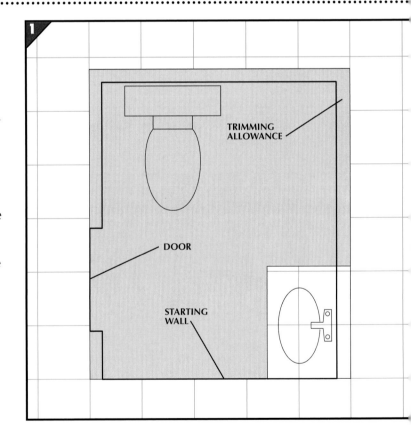

TRIMMING ALLOWANCE

DOOR

STARTING WALL

2. Cutting the carpet.

◆ Place the carpet, backing side up, on a work surface.

◆ Set a cutting board under an edge of the carpet, then lay a metal yardstick alongside the selvage—the tightly-woven edge—and trim it off with a carpet knife *(photograph)*. Cut off the other selvages the same way.

◆ With the yardstick and a felt-tipped marker, transfer the carpet outline from the graph paper onto the backing, converting it to full scale.

◆ With the carpet knife and yardstick, cut along the lines *(right)*—change the blade when the knife begins to drag.

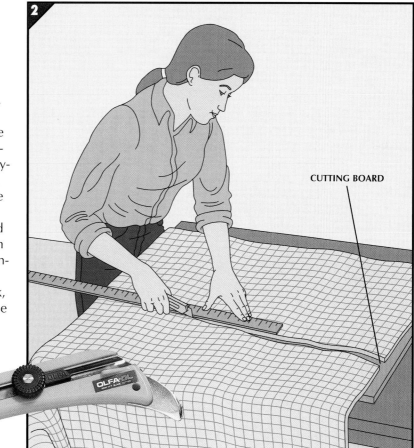

CUTTING BOARD

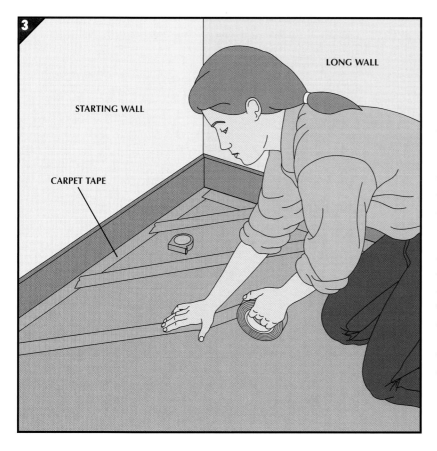

LONG WALL

STARTING WALL

CARPET TAPE

3. Positioning the tape.

◆ Place the end of a roll of double-sided carpet tape sticky-side down in the corner between the starting wall and the long wall. Unroll the tape, pressing it down and aligning an edge with the starting wall. Cut the tape at the end of the wall.

◆ Apply tape along the long wall, laying down two strips of tape side by side at the door threshold.

◆ Continue taping around the perimeter of the floor.

◆ Beginning at the corner between the starting and long walls, stick down diagonal strips of tape at one-foot intervals across the floor *(left)*. Stop when you reach the toilet and vanity or pedestal sink.

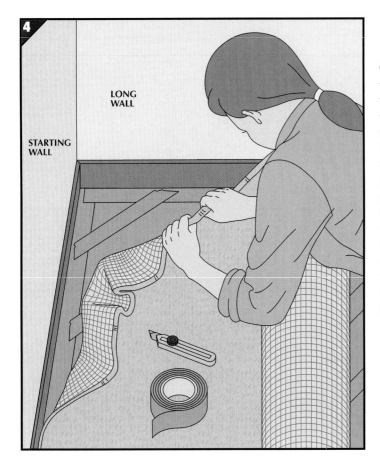

4. Laying the carpet.

◆ Pull off the tape's paper covering on the strip along the starting wall.

◆ Unroll a short length of carpet, position its trimmed edge against the starting wall and on the exposed tape *(left)*, with the 3- to 4-inch trimming allowance riding up the long wall. Press the carpet down on the tape along the starting wall.

◆ Slowly unroll the carpet, removing the paper covering on the diagonal strips of tape and on the strip along the long wall as you go. Smooth and press down on the carpet to make solid contact between it and the tape.

5. Trimming along walls.

◆ Along the edge of the long wall, press the carpet onto the tape and, with the carpet knife, trim along the line between the floor and the wall *(right)*.

◆ At the doorway, cut the carpet flush with the threshold.

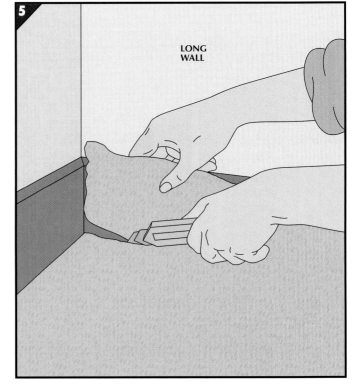

6. Fitting around fixtures.

◆ Smooth the carpet up to the toilet or other fixture and fold it back.

◆ Slide a cutting board into the fold, then make a cut in the carpet that is the mirror image of the contour of the fixture's front edge.

◆ Make a straight cut from the center of the first cut to the edge of the folded carpet *(right),* creating two flaps.

◆ Lay the flaps around the side of the fixture *(inset)* and trim them to fit.

◆ Lift the flaps, apply tape around the fixture, and press the carpet into place.

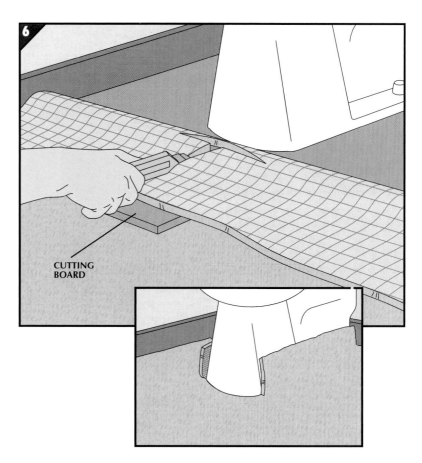

CUTTING BOARD

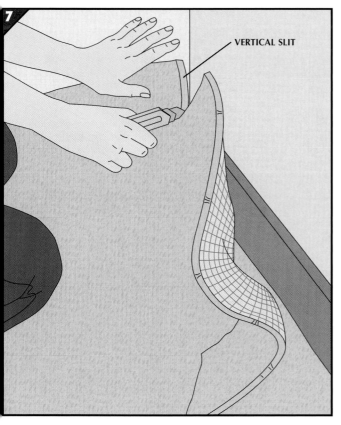

VERTICAL SLIT

7. Finishing the job.

◆ Work around the perimeter of the room, pressing the loose carpet edges onto the tape as you go.

◆ Just before reaching each corner, press the carpet against the wall and make a vertical slit in line with the corner *(left).*

◆ Cut an additional piece of carpet for each area of the floor not covered by the main one, making sure the pile direction of these strips will match that of the main section.

◆ Tape down each additional piece of carpet individually.

A Wall of Mirrors

Mirrors can make a small room appear more spacious. You can cover one wall completely with mirror panels, or you can install them on adjacent walls as a two-piece mirror that permits side views.

Choosing a Type: Good-quality mirrors in large panels or small beveled units are more suited to a bathroom than the less-expensive mirror tiles. The tiles do not provide a sufficiently clear reflection for use in a bathroom, and the double-sided tape that affixes them may loosen in a humid environment.

Mounting Mirrors: You can mount mirrors wall to wall and floor to ceiling, but walls frequently are not perfectly square at the corners. To simplify the installation, leave a narrow border of uncovered wall.
   Small beveled mirrors are typically installed with metal J-channels and a special mastic that will not react with the silver backing *(below and opposite)*. Since mastic results in a permanent installation, use a grid of T-shaped channels instead if you think you may want to remove the mirrors in the future. For large panels, use J-clips *(page 22)*.

 **TOOLS**

	Electric drill
	Hammer
Hacksaw	Screwdriver
File	Straightedge
Carpenter's level	Paint paddle

MATERIALS

	J-clips
	Adjustable top clips
Drop cloth	Wallboard nails
Mirror panels	($1\frac{1}{4}$")
Masking tape	Flat-head screws
Felt	($1\frac{1}{4}$")
Mirror mastic	Hollow-wall
J-channels	anchors

 SAFETY TIPS

Wear work gloves to protect your hands from sharp edges and to shield the mirror backing from salts and oils on your skin.

MOUNTING BEVELED REFLECTIVE PANELS

1. Laying a dry run.
◆ On a drop cloth or carpet, lay out the panels as they will be placed on the wall.
◆ To cushion the edges and pad the joints between the panels, lift each piece and affix a strip of $\frac{1}{2}$-inch masking tape along the edges below the bevels *(right)*, folding the excess onto the back of the mirror *(inset)*.

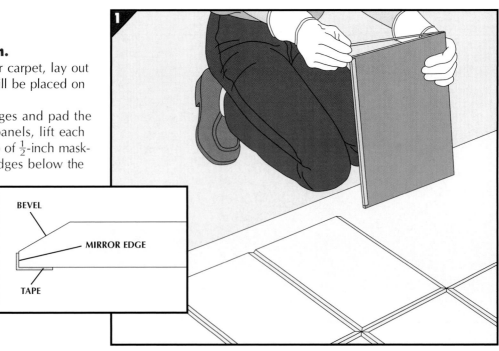

BEVEL

MIRROR EDGE

TAPE

2. Cutting J-channel.

◆ Measure the total length of the bottom edges of the panels as they lie on the floor.

◆ Fit a piece of metal J-channel along the edge of a worktable, clamp it in place, and cut it to this length with a hacksaw *(right)*.

◆ Cut another piece in the same way, then round the ends of the channels at the top corners with a file.

◆ With a carpenter's level, mark level guidelines on the wall to indicate the top and bottom of the area to be mirrored.

◆ Position a length of J-channel along the bottom guideline and fasten it to the wall with $1\frac{1}{4}$-inch wallboard nails driven into holes drilled every 12 inches. Cover the nailheads with masking tape to protect the mirror backing, and glue a 1-inch-long pad of felt to the channel every 4 inches *(inset)*.

◆ Fasten a second J-channel along the top guideline.

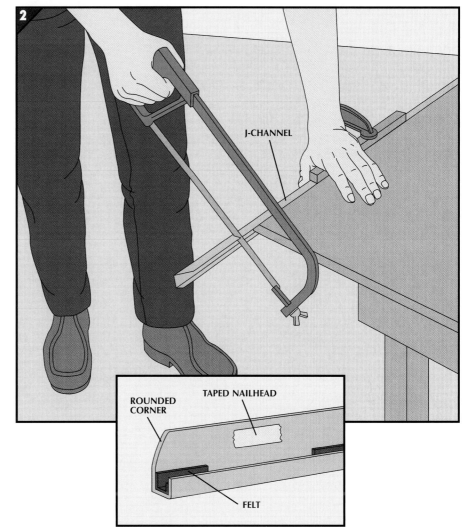

J-CHANNEL

ROUNDED CORNER

TAPED NAILHEAD

FELT

3. Applying mirror mastic.

◆ Turn the first mirror panel over and lay it flat on a drop cloth.

◆ With a wooden paint paddle or a smooth scrap of wood, daub mastic onto the mirror backing, applying four pats roughly $1\frac{1}{2}$ inches square and $\frac{7}{8}$ inches thick for every square foot of mirror *(left)*. To prevent leakage, keep the cement at least $2\frac{1}{2}$ inches from the mirror edges. If the mastic begins to harden on the daubing stick, discard the stick and use a new one.

4. Installing the panels.

◆ Set the first mirror panel into one end of the J-channel, applying uniform pressure to the surface until the mastic is distributed and the back of the panel is about $\frac{1}{4}$ inch from the wall *(right)*.

◆ Complete the bottom row of panels, then install the remaining rows, setting the mirrors end to end and edge to edge. When you reach the top row, slip the mirrors into the top J-channel.

◆ After all the panels are in place, run a padded straightedge over them to flatten and even the surface.

SECURING LARGER MIRRORS

Installing bottom supports.

◆ With a carpenter's level, draw level guidelines on the wall at the planned height of the bottom and top of the mirror panels.

◆ Along each line, mark the edges of the mirror panels and stud locations within the area to be paneled.

◆ With $1\frac{1}{4}$-inch flat-headed screws that fit the holes in the hardware, install a J-clip at each stud location along the bottom guideline *(inset)*. With hollow-wall anchors *(photograph)*, install a second J-clip for each panel.

◆ Pad the J-clips with pieces of felt and cover the screwheads with masking tape.

◆ Install adjustable clips along the top guideline in the same way and pad the screwheads.

◆ With a helper, lift the first panel into position, tilting the top away from the wall and setting the bottom in the first two J-clips. Turn the adjustable clips at the top upward and put the mirror in place, then turn the clips back.

◆ Install the remaining panels the same way *(right)*, butting them edge to edge.

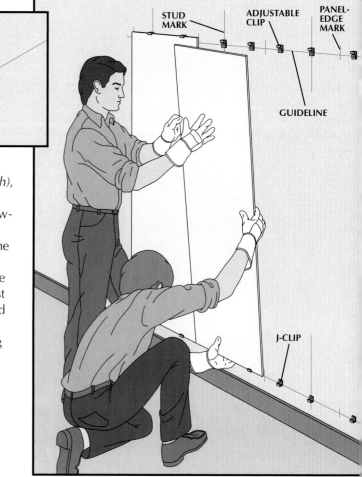

STUD MARK

ADJUSTABLE CLIP

PANEL-EDGE MARK

GUIDELINE

J-CLIP

The fixtures on these pages frame a bathroom mirror and give off an even, warm glow that is complimentary. Installing them is a simple matter when they replace old light fixtures and use existing electrical boxes. If you are replacing a single lamp over the mirror, however, the job is a bit more involved *(page 25)*.

Light Kits: New fixtures come with several pieces of hardware, including screws and a mounting strap. You will need to replace the mounting straps on the existing boxes with the ones provided in the light kit.

Grounding Fixtures: Since the metal plates of light strips are quite large, it is especially important that the fixtures be grounded properly. Check the existing cable *(below)* and do not install light strips on an ungrounded circuit.

⚠️ **CAUTION** *Before you begin, turn off power to the circuits at the service panel (page 119) and confirm it is off (page 120).*

⚠️ **CAUTION** *Check for the presence of aluminum wiring and take the necessary safety measures (page 119).*

 TOOLS

Screwdriver	Electric drill
Continuity tester	Hammer
Carpenter's level	Electrician's multipurpose tool

M MATERIALS

Light-strip kits	Wire caps
Wall anchors	Jumper wires

1. Checking for grounding.
♦ Turn off electricity to the circuit *(page 119)*.
♦ Detach the fixture from the electrical box and carefully expose the wires, then check that the power is off *(page 120)*.
♦ Disconnect the wires and set the old fixture aside.
♦ To check for proper grounding of the existing circuit, touch one probe of a continuity tester to the incoming cable's bare-copper ground wire and the other probe to the bare end of the cable's white wire *(right)*. The tester should light; if it does not, or if there is no ground wire in the box, have a qualified electrician ground the circuit.
♦ Unscrew the nut from the threaded nipple and take off the mounting strap.
♦ Using the same procedure, remove the other fixture.

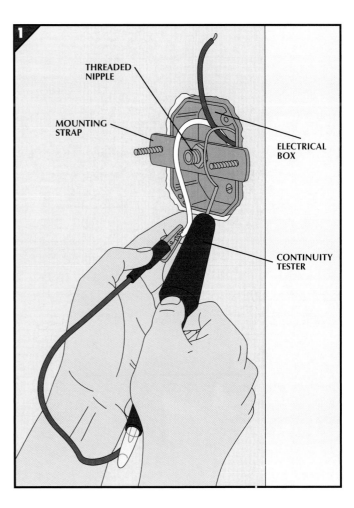

THREADED NIPPLE

MOUNTING STRAP

ELECTRICAL BOX

CONTINUITY TESTER

2. Marking the strip positions.

◆ For each light-strip fixture, make a mark on the wall directly above and below the center of the electrical box.

◆ Holding a carpenter's level plumb at the marks, draw vertical center lines for the fixtures that extend a few inches above and below the mirror *(right)*.

◆ Mark the top or bottom locations of the fixtures on the center lines.

◆ Holding a fixture's back plate in position, mark the screw holes, then drill holes at the marks for anchors of a size suitable for the screws provided.

◆ Tap the anchors into the holes with a hammer so they are seated snugly.

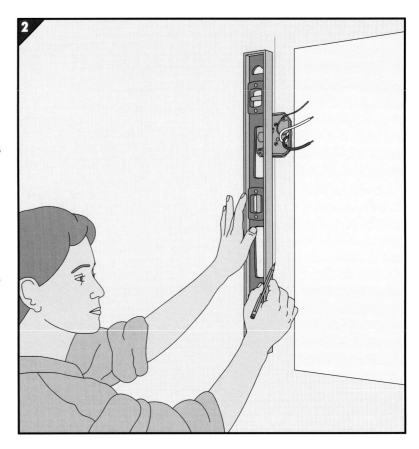

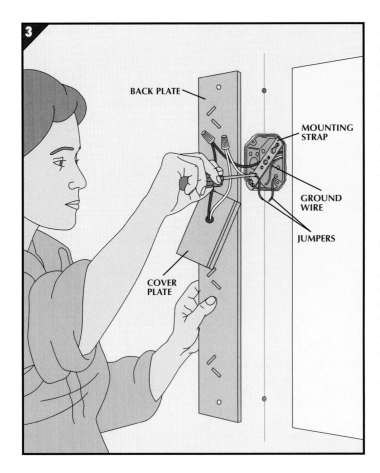

BACK PLATE

MOUNTING STRAP

GROUND WIRE

JUMPERS

COVER PLATE

3. Connecting the wires.

◆ Attach the new fixture's mounting strap to the electrical box.

◆ If the fixture has a cover plate, pass the wires from the back plate through the cover plate.

◆ Holding the back plate near the box, connect the fixture's wires to the wires of the cable or cables in the box with wire caps *(page 122)*—white to white, black to black.

◆ If the box is metal and the fixture has no ground wire, join the bare-copper ground wire of each cable in the box to two short jumper wires in a wire cap. Attach one jumper to the ground screw on the box and the other to the ground screw on the mounting strap *(left)*. When the fixture has a ground wire, cap it with the other ground wires and omit the jumper to the mounting strap. If the box is plastic, omit the jumper to the box.

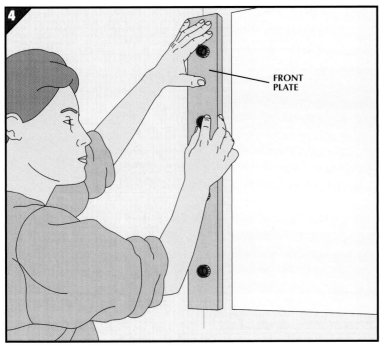

FRONT
PLATE

4. Attaching the strips.

◆ Gently fold the wires into the box, then screw the fixture's cover plate to the mounting strap.

◆ Position the fixture's back plate on the wall and drive screws through it into the anchors.

◆ Snap the front plate onto the back plate and secure it by screwing the socket cups in place *(left)*.

◆ Install the second light strip in the same manner.

◆ Screw light bulbs into the sockets and restore electricity to the circuit.

REPLACING A SINGLE LIGHT FIXTURE WITH TWO SIDE STRIPS

To replace a single fixture above a mirror with light strips at the sides, you will need to route cable from the switch to the first box, then to the second box *(right)*. Turn off power to the circuit, pull the fixture away from the box, and inspect the wiring. If more than one cable enters the box, consult an electrician about wiring the new fixtures. If the box contains only one cable, the fixture is at the end of the circuit and wiring is straightforward. Fasten a box to a stud at each side of the mirror, then disconnect the cable that goes from the switch to the original box and run it into the nearest of the two boxes. Route a second cable from the first to the second box. At the boxes, attach the fixtures' wires to the cable wires as described opposite, Step 3. Cap the original box or remove the box and patch the wallboard.

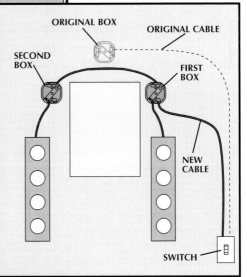

ORIGINAL BOX
ORIGINAL CABLE
SECOND BOX
FIRST BOX
NEW CABLE
SWITCH

Putting in a Pedestal Sink

Replacing a vanity with a pedestal sink is an easy way to create space in a cramped room. And substituting an elegant pedestal-style fixture for a wall-hung sink will give a bathroom a more finished appearance because the pedestal neatly conceals the drainpipe.

Adapting the Plumbing: Since the new sink will not necessarily be the same height or distance from the wall as the old one, you may need to replace the old drain parts to fit the new fixture. Spray metal fittings with a penetrating lubricant several hours before disconnecting them so they will be easier to remove.

For the new drain parts, durable and inexpensive polyvinylchloride (PVC) pipe is a good choice. If the supply tubes are the older, rigid type, you may want to replace them with easy-to-install flexible tubes.

Mounting the New Sink: Basins like the ones shown on these pages are fastened with screws directly to the wall framing; others hook onto metal brackets much like wall-hung models. Both types require blocking between wall studs to support the sink *(page 28)*.

 TOOLS

Pipe wrench
Adjustable
  wrench
Basin wrench
Socket wrench
Pry bar
Hammer
Screwdriver
Stud finder
Carpenter's level
Electric drill
Wallboard saw
Circular saw
Caulking gun

 **MATERIALS**

Pedestal sink
Faucet and stopper
  assemblies
Drain fittings
Flexible supply tubes
2 x 4
Wood screws ($2\frac{1}{2}$"
  No. 8, No. 10)
Lag screws ($\frac{1}{2}$" x $2\frac{1}{2}$")
Silicone caulk
Plumber's putty

 **SAFETY TIPS**

Put on goggles when using a drill, hammer, or saw.

Anatomy of a pedestal sink.

This typical model includes a backless pedestal screwed to the floor, and a basin that is fastened to blocking between the wall studs *(page 28)*. In the basin, a flanged drain piece is joined to a tailpiece with a T-connector, and the tailpiece is connected to a trap. The pop-up stopper assembly moves up and down by means of a lift rod that is linked to the stopper through an extension rod and pivot rod. Faucets fit into holes on 4- or 8-inch centers on top of the sink. Supply tubes for hot and cold water run between the faucets and shutoff valves.

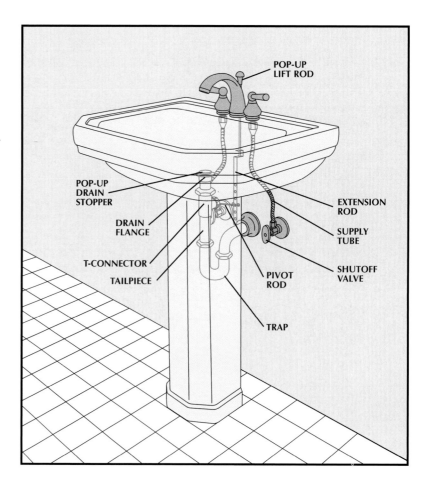

DISCONNECTING THE PLUMBING

Unscrewing the pipes.

◆ Close the shutoff valves and open the faucets to drain the supply pipes. Place a tub under the trap to catch any remaining water as you undo the fittings.

◆ With a pipe wrench, unscrew the slip nuts on each end of the trap, disconnecting it from the tailpiece and the drain extension *(right)*.

◆ Unscrew the tailpiece from the T-connector.

◆ Loosen the escutcheon from the wall and undo the slip nut holding the drain extension in place.

◆ Remove the nuts securing the supply tubes to the shutoff valves.

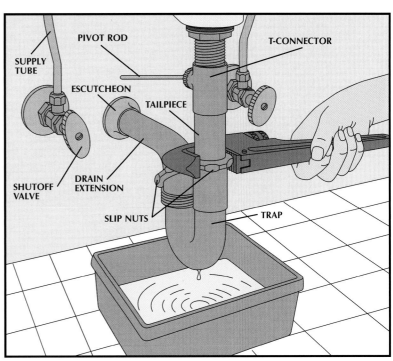

REMOVING THE OLD FIXTURE

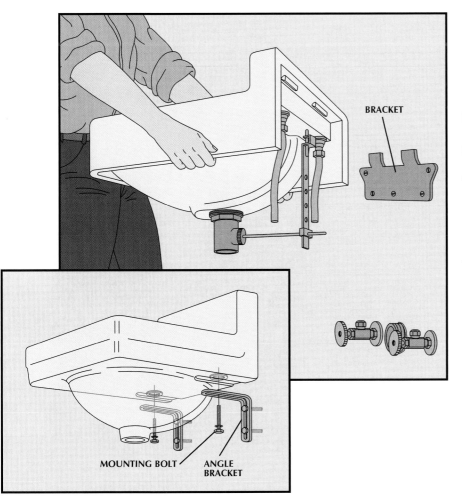

Dismounting a wall-hung sink.

For a bracket-hung sink, simply pull the basin up off its bracket *(left)*.

To detach a sink supported from below by angle brackets *(inset)*, have a helper hold the basin while you unscrew the mounting bolts with a wrench. Set the basin aside and remove the brackets from the wall.

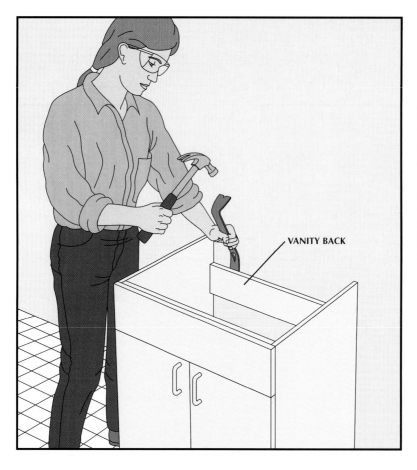

Dismantling a vanity.
◆ Take off any hardware attaching the sink to the wall and lift the sink straight up to free it.
◆ Remove any molding along the sides of the vanity with a pry bar.
◆ If the vanity is nailed to the studs, pry it away from the wall *(left)*. When it is held by screws, remove them and lift it free.

VANITY BACK

INSTALLING THE NEW SINK

1. Adding blocking.
◆ Turn off the power to circuits that run behind the wall *(page 119)*.
◆ With an electronic stud finder, locate and mark the studs on each side of the drainpipe.
◆ Set the pedestal and basin against the wall in the desired position. With a helper holding them in place, mark the height of the basin's screw holes on the wall.
◆ Outline an opening extending about 6 inches above and below the screw-hole marks and to the center of the studs on each side.
◆ Cut out the opening with a wallboard saw, taking care not to cut into wires or pipes that may be routed behind it.
◆ Trim a 2-by-4 to fit between the studs; notch the blocking to fit around any pipes in the way.
◆ Position the blocking between the studs at the screw-hole height and fasten it in place with $2\frac{1}{2}$-inch No. 8 screws driven at an angle *(right)*.
◆ Mark the position of the blocking on the wall at each end of the opening, then patch the hole with wallboard *(pages 63-65)*.

> ⚠ **CAUTION**
> *Before cutting into walls, test for lead and asbestos* (page 43).

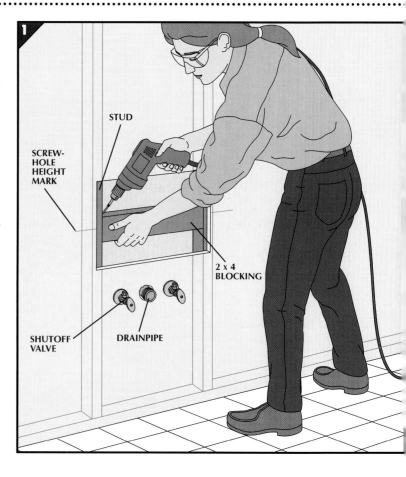

STUD

SCREW-HOLE HEIGHT MARK

2 x 4 BLOCKING

SHUTOFF VALVE

DRAINPIPE

2. Installing the faucet.

Lay the basin down on padding on its front edge and install the faucet in the sink as shown in the inset.

◆ Place a seal washer on the spout shank and push it into its hole in the top of the sink. From under the basin, thread on a rubber washer, a brass washer, and a locknut, making sure that the brass washer's slot faces the back of the sink. Tighten the locknut with a basin wrench.

◆ Slip a locknut and rubber washer on each handle shank and insert the shanks into their holes from under the sink, fitting the hole in the horizontal section of the valve body over the end of the spout shank.

◆ From above, place a rubber ring and an escutcheon on each faucet shank, then tighten the locknuts on the handle shanks with a basin wrench *(right)*.

◆ Add the faucet handles.

VALVE BODY

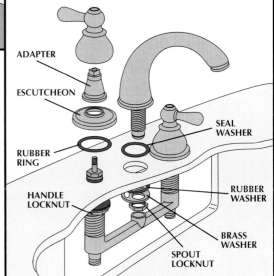

ADAPTER

ESCUTCHEON

SEAL WASHER

RUBBER RING

HANDLE LOCKNUT

RUBBER WASHER

SPOUT LOCKNUT

BRASS WASHER

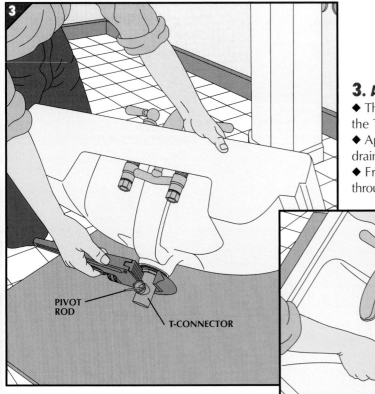

PIVOT ROD

T-CONNECTOR

SLOT

STOPPER

3. Adding the drain.

◆ Thread the locknut, washer, and gasket over the top of the T-connector.

◆ Apply a bead of plumber's putty to the underside of the drain flange.

◆ From the bottom of the sink, push the T-connector up through the drain hole; from inside the sink, thread the flange down onto the T-connector.

◆ Keeping the T-connector's pivot-rod hole pointed toward the back of the sink, tighten the locknut securely with a pipe wrench *(left)*.

◆ From inside the sink, lower the stopper into the T-connector, ensuring that the slot at the bottom is pointed toward the back of the sink *(inset)*.

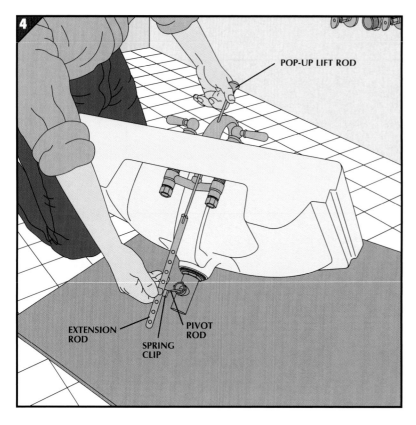

POP-UP LIFT ROD

EXTENSION
ROD
SPRING
CLIP
PIVOT
ROD

4. Installing the pop-up.

◆ Drop the pop-up lift rod through the hole in the spout, then slip the extension rod onto the end of the lift rod and tighten the thumbscrew.

◆ Squeeze both ends of the spring clip together, then slide the clip up the extension rod until you can slip the pivot rod through the clip and into one of the holes in the extension rod (left). Release the clip.

◆ If the drain stopper is too high or low in the sink, loosen the thumbscrew to move the extension rod up or down the length of the pivot rod.

5. Test-fitting the plumbing.

◆ Thread the tailpiece loosely by hand into the T-connector.

◆ Push a drain extension into the drain-pipe in the wall and hand-tighten the slip nut (right).

◆ Move the pedestal and basin into the desired position.

◆ Test-fit the trap by connecting it to the tailpiece and drain extension. If necessary, remove the tailpiece or the drain extension and trim it to length.

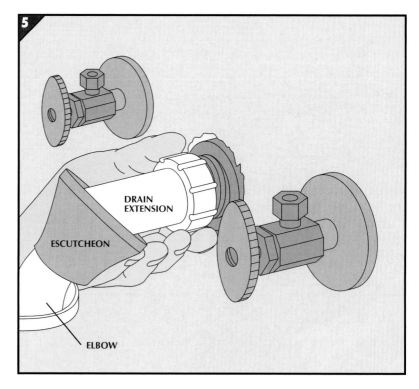

DRAIN
EXTENSION

ESCUTCHEON

ELBOW

6. Marking the screw holes.

◆ Without moving the sink from its position in Step 5, place a level on top of the basin. Have a helper hold the basin level.

◆ Mark the sink's screw holes on the wall *(right)*. Then, mark the pedestal lag-screw holes on the floor.

◆ Set the sink aside.

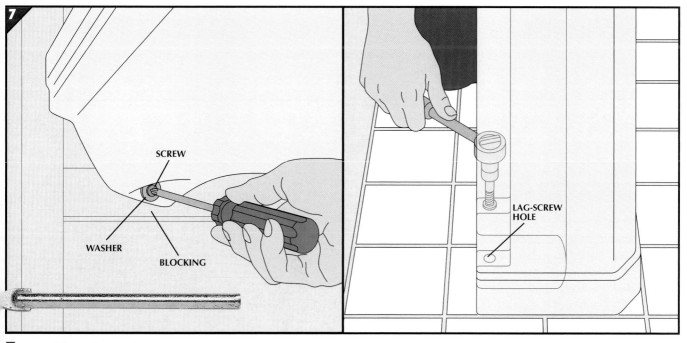

SCREW

WASHER

BLOCKING

LAG-SCREW HOLE

7. Attaching the pedestal and basin.

◆ Drill a pilot hole in the wall blocking for a $2\frac{1}{2}$-inch No. 10 screw at each mark.

◆ Drill holes into the floor for $\frac{1}{2}$- by 2-inch lag screws. With ceramic-tiled floors, use a tile drill bit *(photograph)*.

◆ Reposition the pedestal and basin.

◆ Fix the basin to the wall with screws and washers, taking care not to overtighten them *(above, left)*.

◆ With a socket wrench, fasten the pedestal to the floor with lag screws and washers *(above, right)*, also being careful not to overtighten them.

◆ Reverse the procedure on page 27 to permanently install the plumbing fittings.

◆ Connect flexible supply tubes to the sink faucets and shutoff valves.

◆ Turn on the water and check for leaks, then apply a bead of silicone caulk at the joint between the basin and pedestal.

Putting in a toilet that matches the sink in style and color is an excellent way to unify the decor of a bathroom.

Choosing a Model: Standard two-piece toilets are available in a range of shapes and colors. For a modern look, you can install a low-profile one-piece unit. Or, for an old-fashioned decorating scheme, a toilet with a wall-mounted tank is another option.

Replacement: You can generally use the existing floor flange and drainpipe. If the flange is cracked or broken, however, have a plumber replace it before you install the new toilet. To make sure the new toilet has the correct "footprint" for the flange location, measure from the wall to the center of the bolts that secure the toilet to the floor. The standard measurement is 12 inches, but toilets with 10- or 14-inch footprints are also available. Flexible supply tubes come in various lengths so you should have little difficulty finding one that fits.

⚠️ **CAUTION** *Take care not to over-tighten the bolts that hold the toilet tank to the bowl and the bowl to the floor—a too-tight connection may crack the porcelain.*

 TOOLS

Sponge
Adjustable
   wrench
Socket wrench
Screwdriver
Putty knife
Hacksaw
Caulking gun

 **MATERIALS**

Toilet
Rags
Wax gasket
Silicone caulk
Flexible supply tube

REMOVING THE OLD FIXTURE

1. Disconnecting the water supply.
◆ Close the shutoff valve on the water-supply tube.
◆ Flush the toilet, then sponge the water from the tank and bail or plunge as much as possible from the bowl.
◆ Unscrew the end of the water supply tube at the toilet tank *(right)*.

If the supply tube is the rigid type, re-move the tank *(opposite, Step 2)*, then disconnect the tube at the shutoff valve.

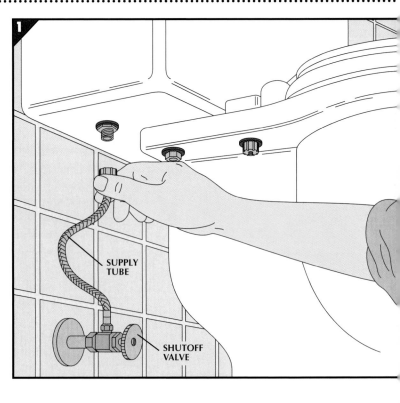

SUPPLY
TUBE

SHUTOFF
VALVE

2. Removing the toilet.

◆ For a two-piece toilet with a bowl-mounted tank, unscrew the nuts under the bowl's back rim with a socket wrench *(right)*—use a screwdriver inside the tank, if necessary, to keep the bolt heads from turning. Lift the tank free of the bowl and set it aside. If the tank is wall-mounted, take off the L-shaped pipe connecting it to the bowl by loosening the slip nuts at each end; then, remove the screws or bolts fastening the tank to the wall.
◆ Pry the caps off the bolts that anchor the bowl to the floor, then undo the nuts.
◆ Rock the bowl gently to break the seal between the toilet and flange, then lift the bowl off the bolts.

Take out a one-piece toilet as you would the bowl of a two-piece model.

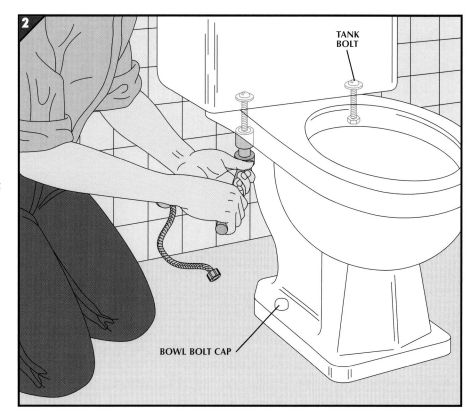

TANK BOLT

BOWL BOLT CAP

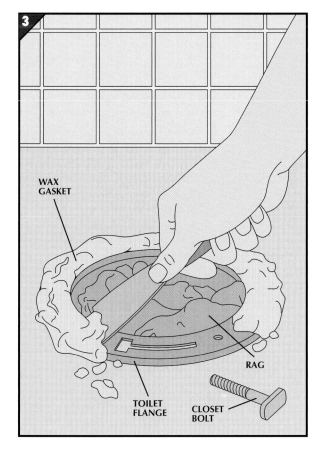

WAX GASKET

TOILET FLANGE

CLOSET BOLT

RAG

3. Scraping the flange.

◆ Stuff a rag into the toilet drainpipe to block off sewer gases.
◆ Slide the closet bolts out of the slots in the toilet flange.
◆ Scrape away the wax gasket with a putty knife *(left)*.
◆ Inspect the flange *(photograph)*; if it is cracked or otherwise damaged, have a plumber replace it.

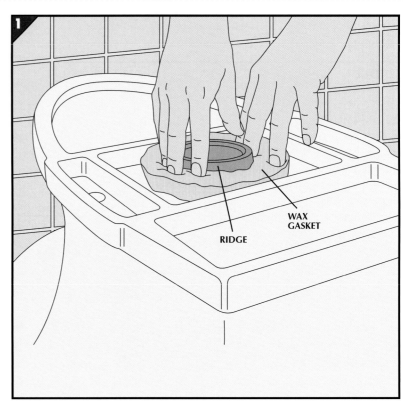

1. Attaching the wax gasket.

◆ Turn the new toilet bowl upside down on a padded surface.

◆ Slip a wax gasket onto the ridge around the bowl's waste hole and press it against the bowl bottom *(right)*.

WAX GASKET

RIDGE

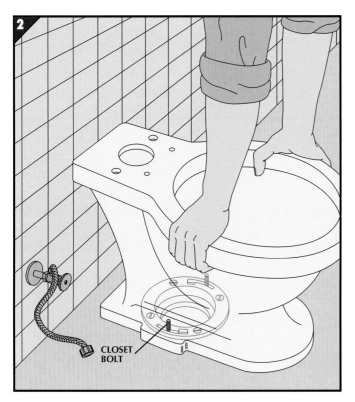

CLOSET BOLT

2. Setting the bowl.

◆ Slide a new closet bolt into each flange slot, positioning the bolts equidistant from the wall.

◆ Lower the bowl onto the bolts *(left)* and press down firmly, rocking the bowl slightly. Avoid raising the bowl off the floor again since this will break the seal between the toilet and the drain.

◆ Level the bowl from side to side and front to back. If necessary, shim it by placing copper or brass washers into gaps at the floor without lifting it up.

◆ If you are using plastic bolt caps, slip a cap base onto each bolt, followed by a metal washer and a nut. Finger-tighten the nuts, then turn each one with a wrench until it is just snug. Trim the bolts with a hacksaw and snap the bolt caps into place. Secure porcelain caps with dabs of caulk.

3. Installing the tank.

◆ Set the tank-to-bowl gasket into position on the bowl.

◆ Lower the tank into place on the bowl so the bolt holes align, as shown at right. Insert tank bolts with rubber washers into the base of the tank and tighten the bolts, taking care not to overtighten them.

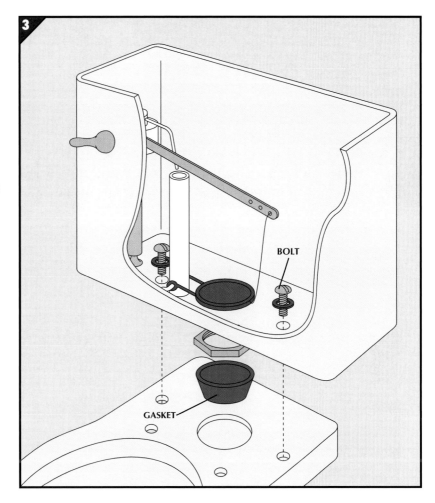

4. Reattaching the supply tubes.

◆ Install the toilet seat and cover.

◆ Attach the supply tube to the toilet tank (left), taking care not to overtighten the nuts.

◆ Open the valve, flush the toilet, and check for leaks. If there are any, tighten the nuts a fraction of a turn at a time with an adjustable wrench until the leaks stop.

The Family Bath

A well-designed family bathroom serves the needs of the whole household efficiently. Space-saving storage ideas include an oversize medicine cabinet recessed into the wall, and a laundry bin built into an existing linen closet. A few added features such as a double-sink vanity and a wall that divides task areas let more than one family member use the room simultaneously.

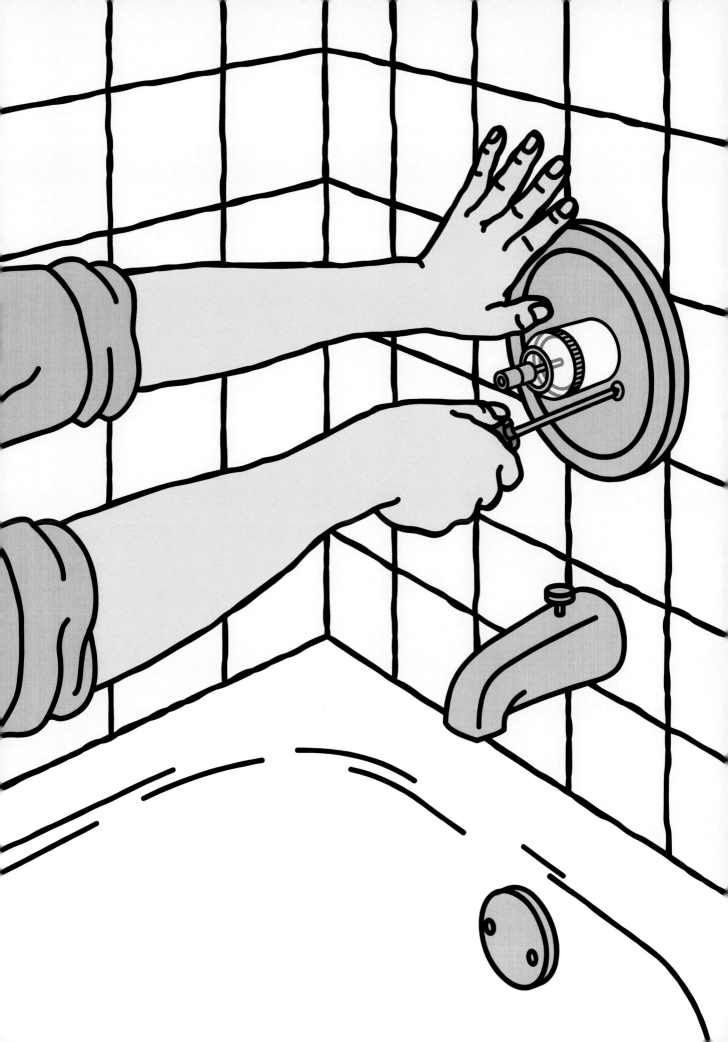

The Family Bathroom: Something for Everyone

Achieving a balance between practicality and style is one of the biggest challenges in redesigning a family bathroom—especially when household members' requirements are widely varied. The secret to success is thorough planning. Before you start to remodel, take full inventory of everyone's needs—young and old, short and tall—and make a list of possible design and furnishing solutions. You may find it helpful to consult with a professional when you are assessing the feasibility of your ideas. A consultant can also introduce you to products on the market that you may not be aware of.

A high-traffic area of the house, the family bathroom is often of only modest size. Even so, there are ways to design the existing space so it can accommodate more than one person at a time. Make a sketch of the room, dividing it into separate task stations to see how you might arrange it to be more efficient. Where space permits, you can build

A half-height privacy wall, built at a convenient level and smartly capped with contrasting tile, doubles as a handy shelf and provides a place to hang an extra towel rack.

These twin sinks have ample room below for a step-up bench that puts them in reach of small children. The short countertop between the basins can be used for toiletries and towels.

a full or half-height dividing wall *(pages 60-65)* to define a certain area or to offer more privacy while two people are in the room.

Perhaps the most practical addition to any family bathroom is a double sink *(pages 50-53)*. This fixture can take some of the pressure off workday-morning rush hours, or serve as an aid in teaching and supervising youngsters in daily tasks such as brushing teeth. To provide access to tod-

dlers, you can add a simple portable step-up bench under the sink or a pull-out drawer step in the bottom of a double-sink vanity.

A few user-friendly features can make baths and showers more accessible for all. Lever-style faucet handles that require little grip strength are helpful for young, elderly, or handicapped family members. Scald-proof shower faucets *(pages 54-55)* and variable-height shower heads are prac-

A slide-out organizer expands this vanity's usable storage area and puts everything within easy reach.

ter of soiled towels and articles of clothing, you can build a laundry bin into the often wasted space at the bottom of a bathroom linen closet *(pages 56-59)*.

When choosing finish materials for the family bath, keep in mind that durability is as important as appearance. One-piece, cast-polymer countertops and sink basins are easy to clean but prone to scratches, while a solid-surface counter is virtually indestructible. Such tops cost more than their cast-polymer or plastic-laminate counterparts, but are well worth it in a busy bathroom.

Ceramic tiles, known for their durability and decorative versatility, are still a prac-

tical additions that increase bathing safety and convenience.

When space is limited, it is worth the time and expense to plan and build more efficient means of storing toiletries, towels, and bath items. Opening walls and reclaiming the space between studs, for instance, can provide a few precious inches behind a sink to accommodate a deeper medicine cabinet *(pages 42-49)*. Or, you can add a tiled shelf recessed into the wall within reach of the bathtub or shower to create a convenient place to store shampoo, soap, and back scrubbers. To keep the floor free of the clut-

A shallow basin, with plumbing set out of the way, permits wheelchair clearance under a lavatory.

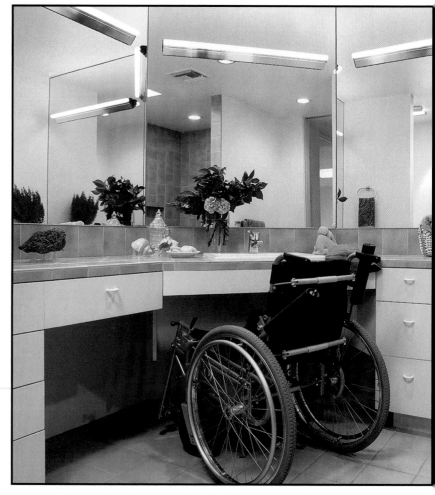

tical, affordable favorite for countertops, walls, and floor. A backsplash of tile can be more than just a protective element—with a little imagination, it can become a decorative highlight echoing other facets of the design scheme.

Flooring comes in a wide variety of materials and design styles. When you are deciding on a type, factor in safety among the other considerations. Nonslip matte or textured-finish tiles, for example, are just as attractive as glossy tiles and cost less than natural textured stone.

Lighting, too, is important. Use windows to their best advantage by covering them with treatments that let in as much light as possible. Panes of diffused glass or stained glass are good choices, as are blinds or curtains that are easy to open and close. Specific task areas that require good lighting are usually best served by halogen or incandescent fixtures.

This oversized, recessed medicine cabinet provides ample space for an entire family to store bath needs. Its large, three-piece mirror helps give a spacious feel to the room.

A Medicine Cabinet Built Into the Wall

Inside a family bathroom, where every inch of space is precious, a custom-built medicine cabinet recessed in a wall solves several problems at once. The cabinet can be built larger and deeper than factory-made models, and its mirror can be bigger and brighter.

Framing the Mirror: Order a mirror of the desired size; specify a safety backing, which both seals against moisture and makes the glass shatter-resistant. Then, have a frame shop cut a standard metal picture frame to fit the mirror. Alternatively, you can back the mirror with plywood and frame it with wood or metal J-channel molding designed for mirrors *(page 21)*, or you can

fasten a beveled mirror directly to plywood backing with no frame.

Preparing the Opening: Constructing a recessed cabinet requires cutting a hole in the wall and removing sections of one or two studs, then patching the wall. Removing one or two studs from nonbearing interior walls is safe, but consult an architect or structural engineer before building a cabinet in an exterior wall or in an interior bearing wall. If you must remove a stud that supports a wallboard joint on the other side of the wall, reinforce the joint by substituting $\frac{1}{2}$-inch plywood for the cabinet back and fastening the wallboard to the plywood with short screws.

 TOOLS

Stud finder	Nail set	Electric drill
Carpenter's level	Wallboard saw	Hole-drilling jig
Combination square	Backsaw	C-clamps
Carpenter's square	Circular saw or table saw	Bar clamps
Screwdriver	Hacksaw	Household iron
Hammer	Utility knife	Rasp

 **MATERIALS**

1 x 2s, 1 x 6s, 2 x 4s
Furniture-grade plywood ($\frac{1}{4}$", $\frac{3}{8}$")
Edge banding
Quarter-round molding
Glass mirror ($\frac{1}{4}$")
Metal picture frame ($1\frac{1}{4}$"), spring clips, and tabs
Piano hinge (2")
Magnetic latch
Shelf pins
Common nails ($2\frac{1}{2}$", 3")
Finishing nails (1", $1\frac{1}{2}$")
Wood screws ($\frac{1}{2}$" No. 8)
Pan-head sheet-metal screws ($\frac{1}{4}$", $\frac{5}{8}$" No. 6)
Sandpaper (medium grade)

 **SAFETY TIPS**

Protect your eyes with goggles when using power tools or a hammer.

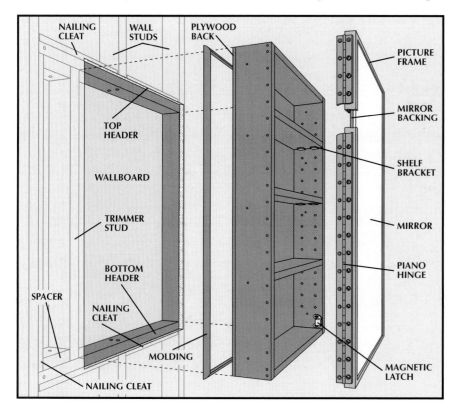

A built-in medicine cabinet.
The oversize medicine cabinet shown here has a frame of 1-by-6s with a plywood back. The cabinet's door, a $1\frac{1}{4}$-inch metal picture frame enclosing a $\frac{1}{4}$-inch mirror and plywood backing, is mounted on one side of the cabinet with a 2-inch-wide piano hinge. The mirror and backing are sized 1 inch wider and 2 inches taller than the cabinet to overlap the top, bottom, and unhinged side. Adjustable 1-by-6 shelves rest on metal brackets whose pins fit into holes drilled on each side of the cabinet. A magnetic latch and metal strike plate hold the door closed. The cabinet is set into a rough frame of 2-by-4 headers at the top and bottom, and a wall stud and a trimmer stud at the sides. One wall stud was cut to accommodate this cabinet, but you can cut away two studs to make a wider unit. Nailing cleats of 1-by-2s support a wallboard patch at the side of the cabinet. Molding hides the joint between the cabinet and the wall.

Figure labels: NAILING CLEAT, WALL STUDS, PLYWOOD BACK, PICTURE FRAME, TOP HEADER, MIRROR BACKING, WALLBOARD, SHELF BRACKET, TRIMMER STUD, MIRROR, BOTTOM HEADER, PIANO HINGE, SPACER, NAILING CLEAT, MOLDING, MAGNETIC LATCH, NAILING CLEAT

PREPARING THE OPENING

1. Removing the wallboard.

◆ With an electronic stud finder, locate and mark the studs behind and to each side of the planned location of the cabinet.

◆ With a carpenter's level, draw a horizontal line $4\frac{1}{2}$ inches above the backsplash or sink top crossing the marked studs.

◆ Measure up $3\frac{1}{2}$ inches more than the height of the cabinet and make a second line.

◆ With a wallboard saw, cut along each line, restarting on the opposite side of any intermediate stud, then make vertical cuts along the inside edges of the two outer studs using each stud as a guide (right).

◆ Break the cutout rectangles of wallboard into pieces with a hammer and tear out the pieces by hand. Pry away any fragments clinging to the studs.

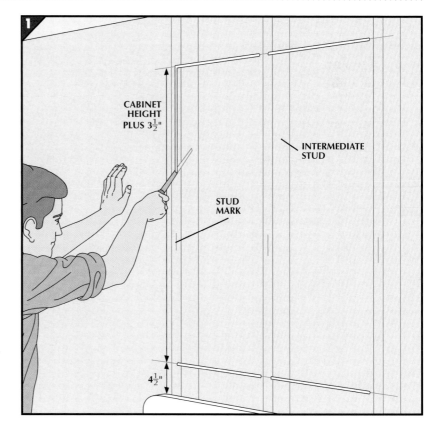

CABINET HEIGHT PLUS $3\frac{1}{2}$"

INTERMEDIATE STUD

STUD MARK

$4\frac{1}{2}$"

2. Freeing the intermediate stud.

◆ Hold a length of 2-by-4 flat against the wallboard at the back of the opening with one edge along the intermediate stud, then strike the 2-by-4 once with a hammer to pop the nails that fasten the wallboard to the stud *(left)*.

◆ Working in the room behind the opening, drive the popped nails through the wallboard into the stud with a hammer and a nail set. Refasten the wallboard to the stud above and below the opening with wallboard screws.

3. Cutting the studs.

◆ With a combination square, draw horizontal lines level with the bottom and top of the opening across the edges of each intermediate stud.

◆ Cut each stud along the lines with a backsaw *(right)*, then pull out the cut pieces.

4. Installing headers.

◆ Cut a 2-by-4 header to fit snugly between the outside studs at the bottom of the opening. To support the wallboard below the opening, nail 1-by-2 cleats to the bottom of the header, leaving gaps for each intermediate stud.

◆ Tap the header into place, cleats downward *(right)*, then fasten it to the intermediate stud with a pair of 3-inch common nails.

◆ Level the header and mark its height on the end studs; then, keeping it level with the marks, toenail it to the outside studs.

◆ Install a top header and cleats in the same way.

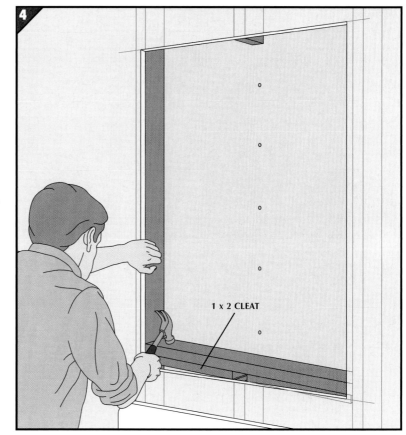

5. Adding a trimmer stud.

◆ Mark the opening's finished width—centered over the sink—on the bottom header.

◆ If a mark is $1\frac{1}{2}$ inches or less from an outside stud, fill the space with strips of plywood nailed to the stud. For a wider gap, first nail a 1-by-2 cleat to the stud, then cut a 2-by-4 trimmer stud to fit snugly between the headers and set it in place, aligning its inner face with the mark.

◆ Cut a 2-by-4 spacer to fit horizontally between the cleat and the trimmer stud, then nail them both to the bottom header *(inset)*.

◆ Plumb the trimmer stud with a carpenter's level and mark its top end on the top header *(left)*. Nail a spacer between the cleat and the trimmer at the top of the opening, then toenail the trimmer to the top header.

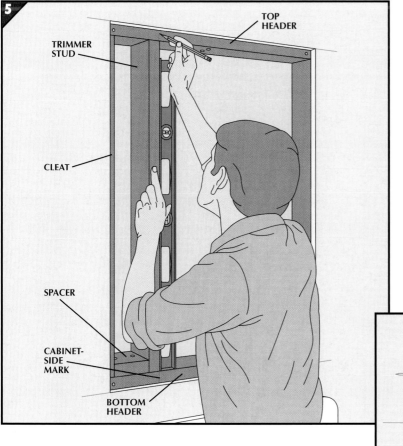

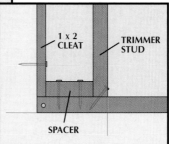

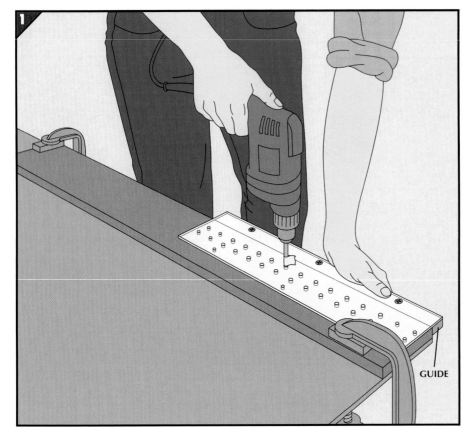

GUIDE

1. Preparing the side pieces.

◆ Cut two 1-by-6s to the planned height of the cabinet.

◆ Secure one of the pieces to a worktable with a pair of C-clamps, protecting it with wood pads.

◆ Fit an electric drill with a $\frac{1}{4}$-inch bit and wrap masking tape around it to mark the drilling depth—the length of a shelf-peg shaft plus the thickness of a commercial hole-drilling jig.

◆ Butt the guide of the hole-drilling jig against the edge of the piece, then select a hole for the top shelf peg and drill into it until the masking tape touches the jig.

◆ Drill all of the holes in the same column (left), then move the jig to the other side of the piece and drill a second row of holes.

◆ Drill the shelf-pin holes in the other 1-by-6 in the same manner.

◆ Cut 1-by-6 top and bottom pieces $1\frac{1}{2}$ inches shorter than the planned width of the cabinet.

TRICKS OF THE TRADE

Extending a Line of Shelf-Pin Holes

The sides of the cabinet may be longer than the hole-drilling jig you are using. To continue a row of shelf-pin holes while keeping their spacing consistent without measuring, use this simple trick. When the last hole in the jig has been drilled, move the jig to the next section, positioning the first hole in the jig over the last hole that you drilled. Slip a shelf pin into the hole, align the jig's guide on the wood, and continue drilling.

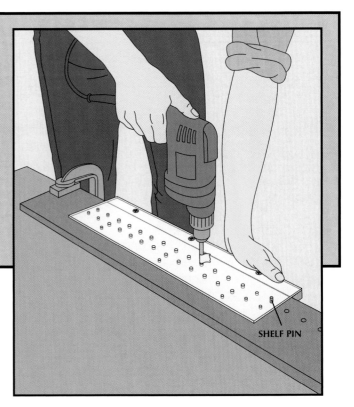

SHELF PIN

2. Applying edge banding.

◆ On a worktable, support one of the cabinet pieces with a pair of bar clamps so that the front edge faces up; protect the piece with wood pads.

◆ Cut a strip of banding slightly longer than the cabinet piece and place the strip on the edge with the adhesive side down.

◆ Set a household iron to HIGH (without steam). Run the hot iron slowly along the edge, pressing the banding ahead of the iron flat with your hand as you work. To prevent scorching the banding, avoid holding the iron in one spot for more than a few seconds.

◆ Applying even pressure, run a small block of wood or hand roller back and forth along the edge.

◆ After the glue has set, trim away excess banding with a rasp (right), then smooth the edges with medium-grade sandpaper.

◆ Apply banding to the remaining cabinet pieces in the same way.

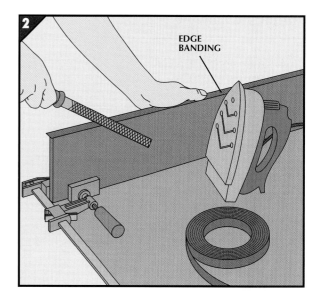

EDGE BANDING

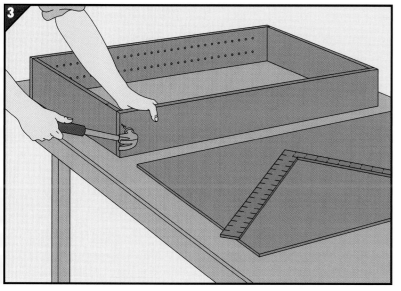

3. Assembling the cabinet.

◆ On a flat work surface, butt the top piece against one of the side pieces. Square the corner with a carpenter's square, then nail the pieces together with a pair of $1\frac{1}{2}$-inch finishing nails.

◆ Butt the other side piece against the top piece, check for square, and nail the pieces together.

◆ Add the bottom piece between the two sides and attach it with a pair of nails through each side (left).

◆ For the back, cut $\frac{1}{4}$-inch furniture-grade plywood to the outside dimensions of the cabinet and nail it to the back of the top, bottom, and sides with 1-inch nails every 6 inches.

4. Making the door.

◆ For the mirror backing, cut a piece of $\frac{1}{4}$-inch furniture-grade plywood 1 inch wider and 2 inches taller than the cabinet.

◆ Set a locking tab atop a plain tab at each end of the long sides of a metal picture frame cut to the correct size (inset).

◆ Slide two tabs together into the narrow rectangular groove along the frame's back and tighten the locking screw. Slide the frame's short sides onto the protruding tabs from one long side; tighten the locking screw for the short sides.

◆ Slip the plywood backing into the frame.

◆ To secure the plywood, insert the metal spring clips supplied with the frame between the plywood and the frame's rear flange (right).

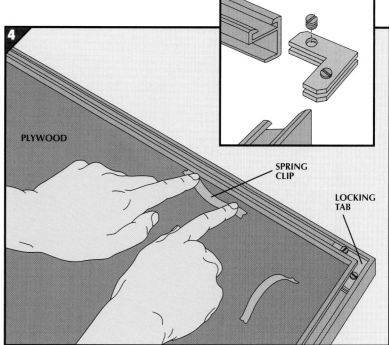

PLYWOOD

SPRING CLIP

LOCKING TAB

MOUNTING THE UNIT

1. Attaching the hinge.

◆ Set the remaining long frame piece on a worktable, its flat edge up and the back of it toward you. Support the piece on a scrap of plywood.

◆ Cut a length of 2-inch-wide piano hinge an inch shorter than the frame piece. Fold the hinge into a right angle and center one leaf on the edge of the piece with the other leaf held against the piece's back and the hinge knuckle pointing outward.

◆ Secure the hinge and frame to the table with C-clamps and wood pads.

◆ Fit an electric drill with a $\frac{3}{32}$-inch bit and drill through the hinge holes and into the frame *(right)*, then fasten the hinge to the frame with $\frac{1}{4}$-inch No. 6 pan-head sheet-metal screws.

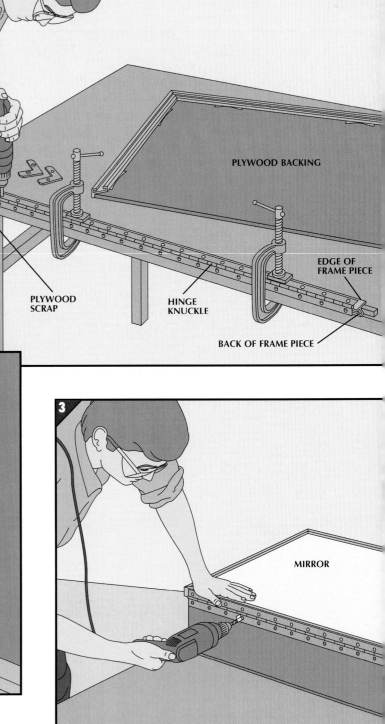

PLYWOOD BACKING

EDGE OF FRAME PIECE

PLYWOOD SCRAP

HINGE KNUCKLE

BACK OF FRAME PIECE

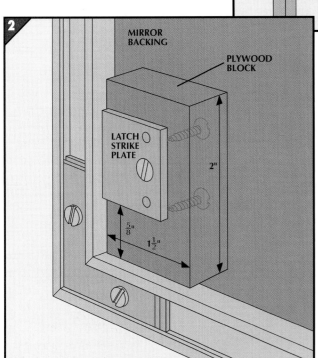

MIRROR BACKING

PLYWOOD BLOCK

LATCH STRIKE PLATE

2"

$\frac{5}{8}$"

$1\frac{1}{2}$"

2. Installing the latch.

◆ In the corner of the frame that will hold the latch, set a $1\frac{1}{2}$- by 2-inch block of $\frac{3}{8}$-inch plywood against the rear surface of the plywood backing.

◆ Drill pilot holes through the backing and into the block for two countersunk $\frac{1}{2}$-inch No. 8 wood screws, then fasten the block to the backing with wood glue and screws.

◆ Place the magnetic latch's metal strike plate vertically on the block, $\frac{5}{8}$ inch from the block's bottom edge, and fasten it with the screw provided *(above)*.

MIRROR

3. Aligning the door.

◆ Slide the mirror into the frame, fit the hinged piece into the frame, and install the spring clips.

◆ Align the door with the cabinet, then fit a drill with a $\frac{3}{32}$-inch drill bit and wrap masking tape $\frac{1}{2}$ inch from its tip.

◆ Drill through the hinge's holes into the cabinet, stopping when the tape reaches the hinge *(above)*.

4. Fastening the cabinet.

◆ Set the cabinet in the opening, then level and plumb it with wood shims placed every 12 to 16 inches.
◆ Fasten the sides of the cabinet to the framing with 2-inch No. 8 wood screws driven through the shims *(right)*.
◆ Check the cabinet again for level and plumb. If it is not perfectly aligned, remove the screws and adjust the shims, then replace the screws.
◆ With a utility knife, cut off the shims flush with the surrounding framing.
◆ Cut wallboard and patch the opening at the side of the cabinet *(pages 63-65)*.

WOOD SHIMS

5. Attaching the door and latch.

◆ With a helper holding the door in place, fasten it to the side of the cabinet through the pre-drilled holes with $\frac{5}{8}$-inch pan-head sheet-metal screws *(left)*.
◆ Hold the magnetic latch for the bottom front of the cabinet side opposite the installed strike plate. Align the magnet in the latch with the cabinet's front edge and screw it in place *(inset)*.
◆ Cut quarter-round molding to fit around the cabinet, mitering the corners, and nail it in place.
◆ From the same stock as the cabinet, cut 1-by-6 shelves $\frac{1}{8}$ inch shorter than the inside dimensions of the cabinet. Apply edge banding to one edge of each shelf *(page 48, Step 2)*. Install the shelves with shelf pins.

Putting in a Double-Sink Vanity

You can shorten rush-hour lineups and create additional storage space by replacing a one-sink vanity with a two-sink model. Be sure the vanity you buy can in fact house two sinks. Some types that have the required counter space for two basins are outfitted with drawers, shelves, and dividers that will interfere with the plumbing needed to serve them.

Placing the Vanity: Before acquiring a new vanity, make sure the bathroom is large enough to accommodate it. A vanity must be a minimum of 48 inches in length to allow for a comfortable and functional two-sink installation. The basins and their openings must be centered in the counter-top, but the vanity itself need not be perfectly centered over the original drain and supply lines. The new plumbing can be adjusted in either direction to reach the new sink positions. The basic plumbing techniques, tools, and materials you'll need to connect the sinks are illustrated on pages 123 to 125.

A Variety of Sinks: Unless you can find an exact replica of your existing sink, purchase a pair of matching new ones. Buy self-rimming basins designed to be set into a vanity countertop, or buy a molded countertop with integral twin sinks.

 TOOLS

Hacksaw or tube cutter
Adjustable wrench

Carpenter's level
Electric drill
Saber saw
Caulking gun

 **MATERIALS**

Twin sinks
Double-sink vanity
Countertop
Faucets and stopper assemblies
Supply pipes and fittings

Shutoff valves
Flexible supply tubes
Drainpipes and fittings
Adjustable traps
Wallboard screws ($2\frac{1}{4}$", No. 6)
Adhesive caulk

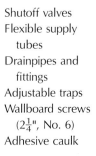 **SAFETY TIPS**

Protect your eyes with goggles and your hands with work gloves when using a propane torch. Put a flame-proof pad behind the work and keep a fire extinguisher nearby.

Plumbing for two sinks.

In the installation at right, a double elbow allows two sinks to drain out through one outlet pipe. An adjustable trap that can swivel at 90 degrees is joined to the tailpiece of each sink with a short drainpipe and a pipe adapter—alternatively, a tailpiece extension could be used. The traps are linked to the double elbow with elbows and straight drainpipes.

The hot- and cold-water supply pipes exit the wall into T-fittings and branch from there into the lines for the two sinks. A pair of shutoff valves is installed at the end of each branch, and flexible supply tubes run from the valves to the faucets. *(In this illustration, the front of the vanity has been removed for clarity.)*

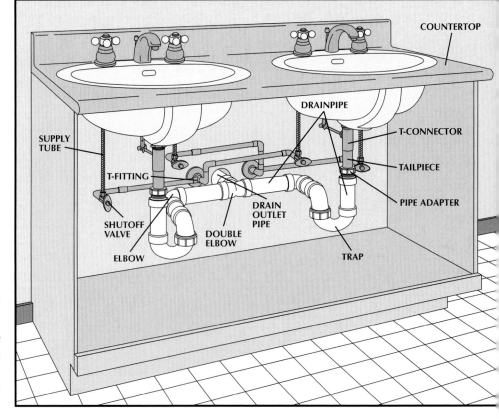

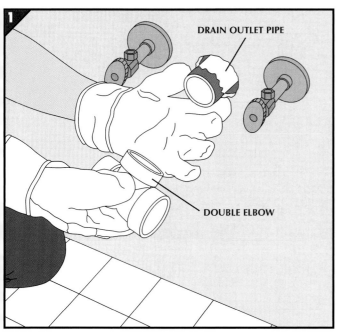

DRAIN OUTLET PIPE

DOUBLE ELBOW

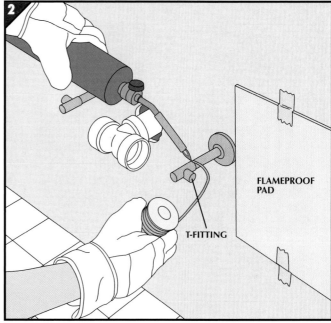

FLAMEPROOF PAD

T-FITTING

1. Installing the drain elbow.

◆ Turn off the water supply at the main shutoff valve and drain the pipes *(page 124)*, then disconnect the supply and drain lines and pull out the old vanity *(pages 27-28)*.

◆ Remove the drain adapter from the outlet pipe, cutting off the pipe a few inches from the wall.

◆ Glue *(page 125)* a double elbow of the proper diameter to the outlet pipe *(above)*.

2. Preparing the supply lines.

◆ With a hacksaw or tube cutter *(page 124)*, sever the supply pipes just behind the shutoff valves.

◆ Prepare a T-fitting for each supply line *(page 125)* and position it on the end of the pipe so that pipes extending from it will be directed toward the two sinks. Protecting the wall with a flameproof pad, solder *(page 125)* the T-fittings to the pipes *(above)*.

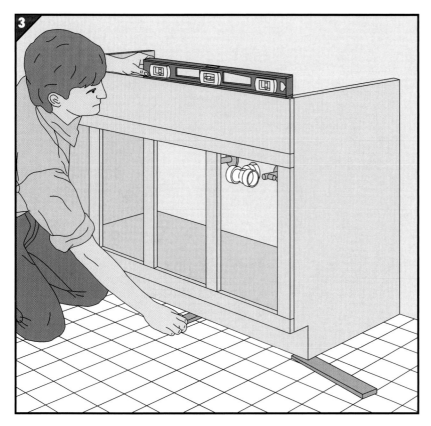

3. Placing the vanity.

◆ Pry off any baseboard on the wall and remove the vanity doors to allow access to the plumbing.

◆ Position the vanity: It need not be perfectly centered around the plumbing, but it will need to be placed so that the plumbing does not conflict with the existing pipes.

◆ Make a line on the wall at each end of the vanity, then set it aside and mark the locations of the studs that fall between the lines.

◆ Reposition the vanity against the wall and level it from end to end by inserting shims under the cabinet *(left)*.

◆ Level the cabinet from front to back by inserting shims between the vanity and the wall.

◆ Drive a $2\frac{1}{4}$-inch No. 6 wallboard screw through the vanity's back plate into each stud.

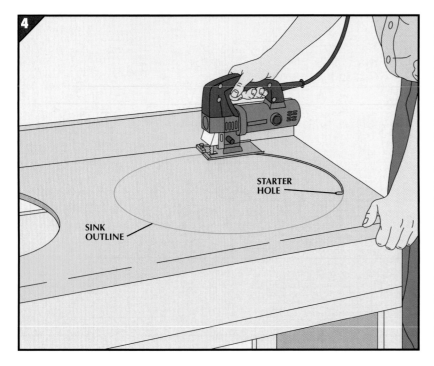

STARTER HOLE

SINK OUTLINE

4. Preparing the countertop.

Buy a plastic-laminated countertop made especially for vanities and cut holes for the sinks. Have the countertop cut large enough to overhang the ends and front of the vanity by 1 inch.

◆ Run a bead of adhesive caulk along the top edges of the cabinet and press the counter firmly into place.

◆ Use the template provided in the sink kit to draw the outline of the basins on the counter, maintaining a border of at least 2 inches between the outline and the edges of the top.

◆ Drill starter holes for the saw blade and make the cuts with a saber saw (left).

Instead of buying a plastic-laminated countertop, you can purchase a top with the sinks molded directly into the material and simply set it in place on a bead of adhesive caulk applied to the top edges of the vanity.

TRICKS OF THE TRADE

Supporting a Sink Cutout

A cutout in a countertop can fall through as you are making the cut, tearing a section of the laminate. To prevent accidents, make starter cuts partway around two sides of the outline. Then, screw wood cleats to the countertop from below so that they cross the cuts as shown. Complete the cutout and remove the cleats.

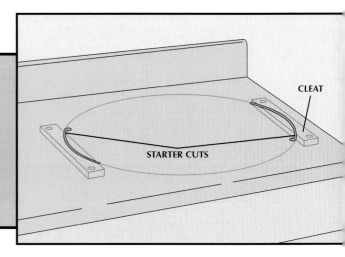

CLEAT

STARTER CUTS

5. Installing the basins.

◆ Fit the two basins with faucets, T-connectors, and pop-up mechanisms (pages 29-30), then attach flexible supply tubes to the faucets.

◆ Lay a bead of adhesive caulk at the perimeter of each sink hole.

◆ Set the basins into their holes (right), pressing them into the caulk. Wipe off any excess caulk immediately.

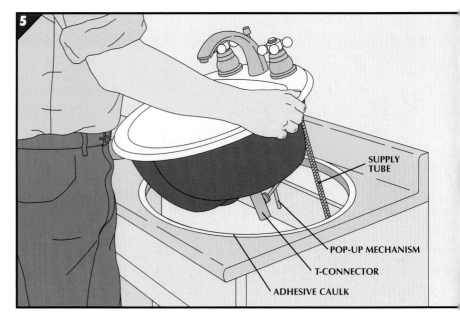

SUPPLY TUBE

POP-UP MECHANISM

T-CONNECTOR

ADHESIVE CAULK

6. Fitting the drain pieces.

◆ Thread a tailpiece into one basin's T-connector.
◆ Temporarily put together a drain assembly: At one end of a trap, connect a 90-degree elbow and a short horizontal pipe; at the other end, attach a short vertical pipe, then a threaded pipe adapter with a slip nut.
◆ Fit the pipe adapter onto the tailpiece and adjust the straight pipes and adapter until the 90-degree elbow is aligned with and slightly higher than the double elbow on the drain outlet.
◆ Measure the distance between the elbows *(right)*, then cut a pipe to that length plus the depth of the fitting sockets and slip it into place.
◆ Fit together the drain pieces for the second basin in the same manner.

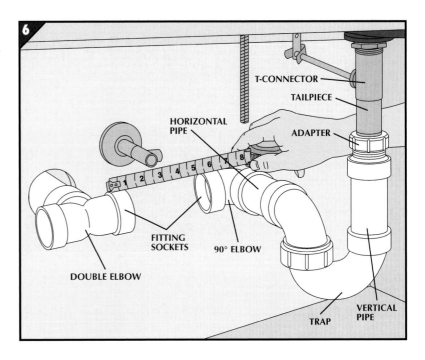

7. Gluing the drain pieces.

Once both installations are correctly put together, mark the pipes where they enter the fittings, then take the assembly apart and glue *(page 125)* the various pipes and fittings together *(left)*.

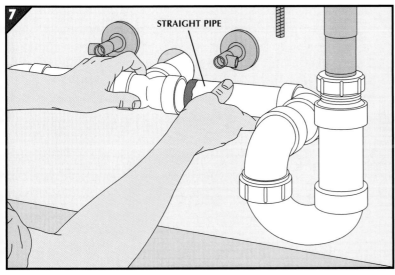

8. Connecting the supply system.

◆ To extend the supply pipes to shutoff valves under each sink, solder *(page 125)* short lengths of pipe and 90-degree elbows to the front openings of the T-fittings on the stub-outs, then add a length of pipe to each elbow, using additional fittings, if needed, to run it to the planned location of the shutoff valve. Solder a length of pipe to the side openings of each T, extending it to the location of the other shutoff valve under the sink.
◆ Solder shutoff valves to the supply pipes.
◆ Fasten the sinks' supply tubes to the shutoff valves, hand-tightening the nuts and giving them a quarter turn with an adjustable wrench *(right)*.
◆ Turn the water back on and check for leaks.
◆ If desired, cover the joints between the vanity and wall with molding.

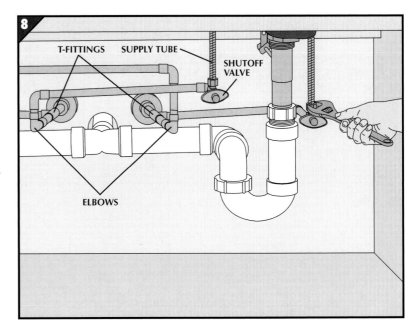

When your bathroom-remodeling project has included installing a new sink *(pages 26-31 and 50-53)* or toilet *(pages 32-35)*, you may want to update the shower hardware as well. If you have a single-handle faucet, you can replace it with a new unit that complements the decor of the bathroom. This is an ideal opportunity to install a pressure-balancing faucet, which will protect your family from scalds as may occur when a toilet is flushed or a washing machine is turned on while someone is showering. Many building codes require this hardware whenever a new faucet is put in. The device is installed in the same way as a regular single-handle faucet *(below and opposite)*. Basic plumbing tools, materials, and techniques are illustrated on pages 123 to 125.

Access to Pipes: Where the tub has no access panel behind the plumbing, you may be able to work from the tub side as shown opposite. If necessary, you can create an access panel by cutting an opening in the wall behind the faucet. Attach cleats to the wall studs and cover the opening with a plywood panel screwed to the cleats.

Two- and Three-Handled Faucets: Pressure-balancing faucets are available only in single-handle models. If you have a two- or three-handle faucet, however, you can have a plumber install a pressure-balancing valve, which is sandwiched between the hot and cold supply pipes.

TOOLS

Screwdriver
Mini-hacksaw

MATERIALS

Pressure-balancing
    faucet
Supply pipe and
    fittings

SAFETY TIPS

Protect your hands with gloves and your eyes with goggles when using a propane torch. While soldering, put a flameproof pad behind the work and keep a fire extinguisher nearby.

INSTALLING A PRESSURE-BALANCING FAUCET

1. Gaining access to the faucet.
◆ Turn off the water supply and drain the lines by opening the faucet *(page 123)*. Close the drain to avoid losing small parts.
◆ Pry off the faucet-handle cap with a screwdriver, then unscrew the faucet handle and set it aside.
◆ Unscrew the escutcheon and take it off the wall *(right)*.

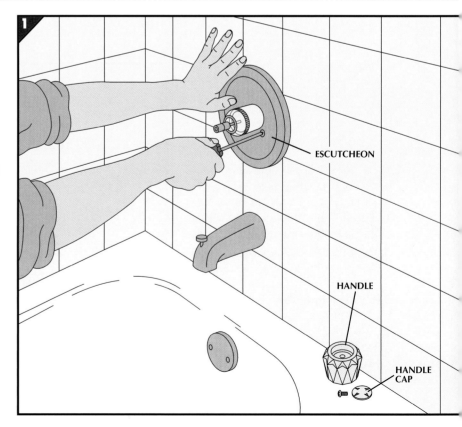

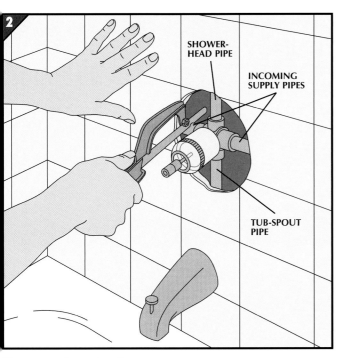

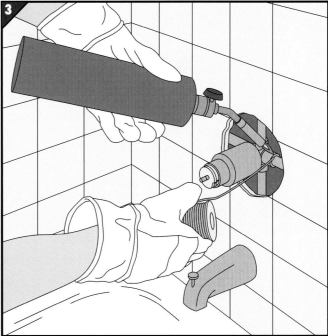

2. Removing the faucet.

If the tub has an access panel on the other side of the wall, work from behind the faucet. Otherwise, create an access hole *(page 54)* or continue working from the tub side.

◆ With a mini-hacksaw, cut the incoming hot- and cold-water pipes, the tub-spout pipe, and the shower-head pipe *(above)*. If you are working at an access panel, there may be enough room to use a pipe cutter instead *(page 124)*.

◆ If the faucet body is clamped to a wooden crosspiece, unscrew the clamps and lift the pipes out of the wall.

3. Installing the new unit.

◆ Measure each section of the old faucet pipes and add $\frac{1}{2}$ inch to their lengths, then cut the new pipes to those measurements and prepare them *(page 124)*.

◆ Insert the pipes into the new faucet body in the same configuration as the old ones.

◆ Position the faucet body and join the pipes with couplings *(page 123)*, then solder *(page 125)* all of the joints *(above)*.

◆ Install the new hardware by reversing the procedure in Step 1 on the page opposite.

TRICKS
OF THE
TRADE

Protecting a Faucet During Soldering

Some shower faucets contain a cartridge with parts that can be damaged by excessive heat, as is generated by a propane torch. If you are inexperienced with soldering and want to ensure that the faucet comes through unscathed, remove the cartridge before you begin. Take off the sleeve and the connector, then grasp the cartridge with pliers and pull it free from the faucet body. When you have finished soldering, let the work cool for a few minutes before you put the cartridge back in place.

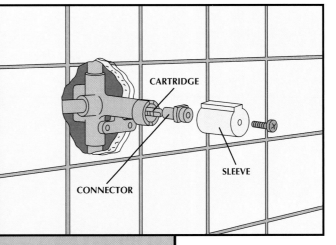

A Convenient Laundry Bin

Keep your laundry out of sight in a bin that tilts open from inside the bathroom linen closet. Easy to build and install, it is a perfect place to store dirty clothing until wash day.

Choosing Materials: Build the unit out of $\frac{3}{4}$-inch furniture-grade plywood finished to match the woodwork in the room or interior of the closet. Cover the exposed edges with banding as described on page 47, Step 2.

Sizing the Bin: The size of the linen closet will dictate the dimensions of the bin—make it as deep as the closet and slightly narrower than the door opening; the most convenient height is 30 to 36 inches. Since the bin should reach to just below the lowest shelf of the closet, you may need to remove or reposition the shelves to accommodate it.

 TOOLS

Circular saw or
   table saw
Electric drill
Hammer
Screwdriver

 **MATERIALS**

Furniture-grade plywood ($\frac{3}{4}$")
1 x 1
Wood screws (1", $1\frac{1}{4}$" No. 8)
Butt hinges (3")
Spring-loaded hook-and-eye catch
Drawer pull

SAFETY TIPS

*Protect your eyes with goggles
when using power tools.*

A tilt-out laundry bin.

The laundry bin at right is $1\frac{1}{2}$ inches narrower than the door opening and $\frac{1}{2}$ inch shorter at the front than the space between the floor and the bottom of the lower shelf in the closet. Its sides are angled at the top to allow them to clear the underside of the shelf as the bin pivots forward on its hinges. A 1-by-1 stop block fastened to the underside of the shelf keeps the back of the bin from falling forward past the shelf. A hook-and-eye catch locks the bin open.

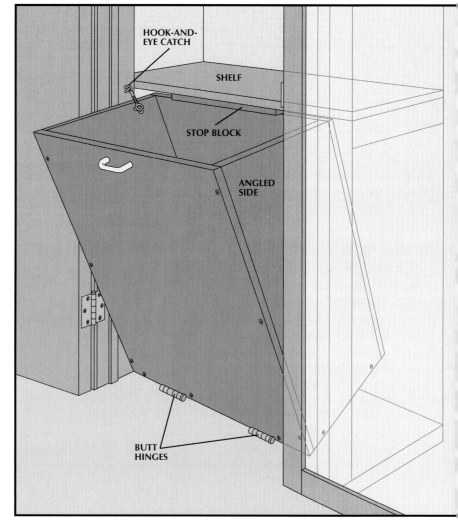

1. Sizing the bin.

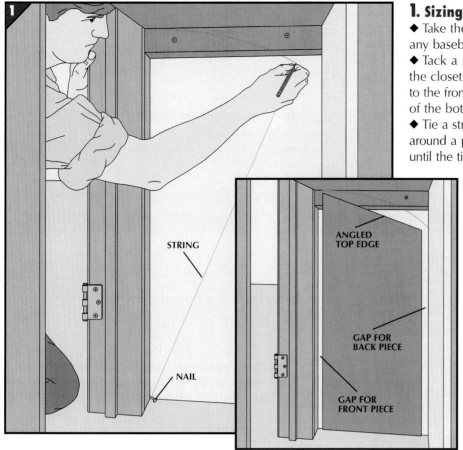

STRING

NAIL

ANGLED
TOP EDGE

GAP FOR
BACK PIECE

GAP FOR
FRONT PIECE

◆ Take the closet door off its hinges and remove any baseboards inside the closet.

◆ Tack a nail into the floor at a front corner of the closet. If the shelves do not reach all the way to the front, place the nail directly below the front of the bottom shelf.

◆ Tie a string to the nail and fasten the other end around a pencil, adjusting the length of the cord until the tip of the pencil touches the bottom front of the lowest shelf.

◆ With the string held taut, trace an arc from the front of the shelf to the back wall of the closet (left).

◆ Measure the distance from the floor to the pencil mark at the front wall and to the mark at the back wall, and cut the side pieces of the bin $\frac{1}{2}$ inch shorter than this height—angling them down from front to back—and $1\frac{1}{2}$ inches narrower than the depth of the closet.

◆ Test-fit the side pieces inside the closet (inset).

2. Building the bin.

◆ Cut the front piece $\frac{1}{2}$ inch shorter than the distance between the floor and the lower closet shelf, and $1\frac{1}{2}$ inches narrower than the width of the doorway. Make the back piece the same width as the front and the height of the short end of the angled side pieces.

◆ Lay a side flat on a worktable and set the front piece against it. Drill pilot holes for three countersunk $1\frac{1}{4}$-inch No. 8 wood screws, then fasten the pieces together. Attach the other side to the front in the same way.

◆ With the unit lying on its front, align the back piece on the sides and fasten it with three screws in each joint.

◆ Cut a bottom panel to the inside dimensions of the assembled unit, and fasten it with a pair of screws through each side and three through the back and front (right).

◆ Attach a drawer pull to the top of the bin's front piece (inset).

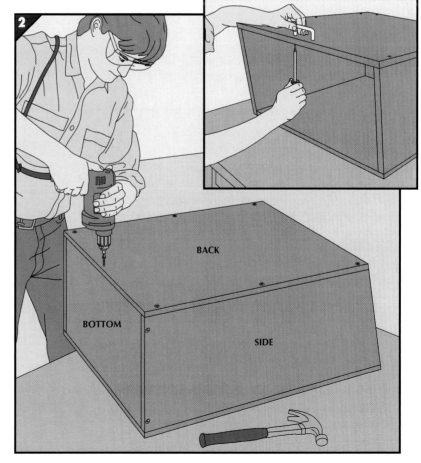

BACK

BOTTOM

SIDE

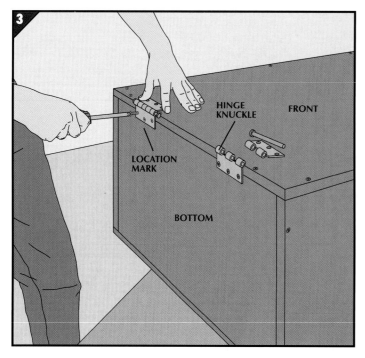

3. Attaching hinges to the bin.

◆ With the assembled unit lying on its back, mark the bottom front of the bin for hinges 6 inches from each end.

◆ Assemble a 3-inch butt hinge and center it over one of the marks on the bin. Make sure the leaf to be attached is flat against the bottom of the bin and that the hinge knuckles clear the surface of the front piece.

◆ Screw the hinge to the bin with the screws provided, then remove the pin and take off the unattached leaf. Fasten the other hinge in the same manner *(left)*.

4. Adding a stop block.

◆ If the lowest shelf in the closet is not secured to its supports, fasten it to them with $1\frac{1}{4}$-inch No. 8 wood screws.

◆ Cut an 18-inch length of 1-by-1 stock as a stop block.

◆ Center the stop on the underside of the lowest shelf, aligning it with the front of the shelf.

◆ Attach the stop to the underside of the shelf with a pair of 1-inch No. 8 wood screws *(right)*.

5. Marking the hinge positions.

◆ Set the assembled bin in the closet, positioning it so there is equal space at the sides. Tilt the bin to make sure it clears the shelf; trim the pieces with a hand plane, if necessary.

◆ With the bin correctly positioned, mark the outline of the two hinges on the floor *(left)*.

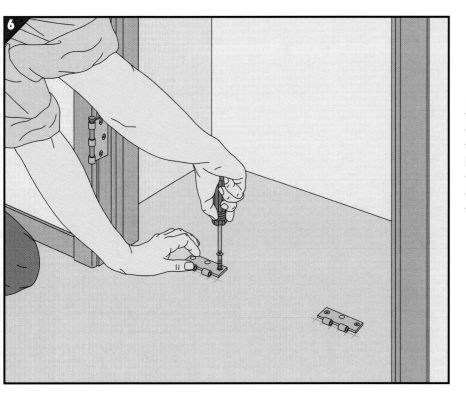

6. Attaching hinges to the floor.

◆ Remove the bin from the closet.
◆ Place an unattached hinge leaf in the outline of the hinge marked on the bin, making sure the knuckles fit between the knuckle marks on the floor.
◆ Fasten the hinges to the floor with the screws provided (left).

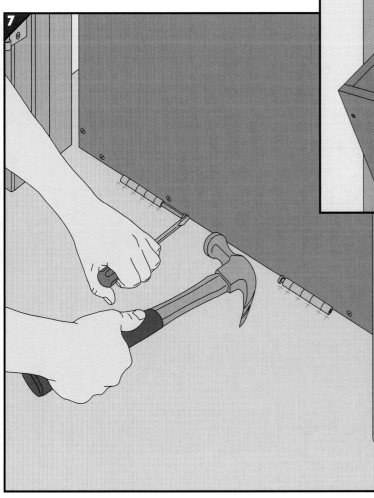

EYE

DOOR-STOP
MOLDING

HOOK

7. Installing the bin.

◆ Place the bin back into the closet and engage the leaves of the hinges.
◆ Tap the hinge pins through the knuckles with a screwdriver and a hammer (left).
◆ Screw the eye of a hook-and-eye catch into the door jamb just below the height of the lower shelf, locating the eye on the inside of the stop molding so that the door can close properly.
◆ Open the bin until the back hits the stop block, then fit the hook of the catch through the eye. Extend the hook until it is taut, unhook it, then screw it into the side of the bin (inset).

A Wall to Divide the Bathroom

Hiding the toilet or bathtub from view with a short dividing wall can increase privacy in a bathroom used by more than one member of the family at a time. A dividing wall also provides a convenient location to hang towel racks or shelving for storage.

Erecting the Wall: The simplest way to build the divider is to assemble it on the ground and lift it into position as shown on page 62. In a small bathroom, however, you may have to build the wall in place by first installing the top plate and soleplate, then toe-nailing the studs to them.

A Moisture-Resistant Covering: Ordinary wallboard can become soft and spongy in the damp environment of a bathroom. For the new wall, use moisture-resistant wallboard, or "greenboard," so named for its green

face paper. The core of this material is saturated with asphalt to repel water. For walls you intend to tile, use cement board instead of greenboard.

Working with Wallboard: Standard wallboard panels measure 4 feet by 8 feet. For a wall longer than 4 feet, hang panels horizontally *(page 63)*; for a wall 4 feet or less, install a single vertical sheet.

To trim the panels, place a wallboard T square at the marked line and cut through the paper with a utility knife. Grasp the edge of the panel on both sides of the cut and snap the short section away from you, breaking it along the cut line. Pull the short section back slightly and make a foot-long slit along the bend on the back of the panel. Snap the short section forward again to break it off, creating a clean, even edge.

 TOOLS

Stud finder
Chalk line
Plumb bob
Combination square
Hammer

Electric drill
Circular saw
Utility knife
Caulking gun
Tin snips
Taping knives

 **MATERIALS**

2 x 4s
Cedar shims
Wallboard ($\frac{1}{2}$")
Common nails ($3\frac{1}{2}$")

Wallboard screws ($1\frac{1}{2}$", 3")
Corner bead
Joint compound
Wallboard adhesive
Paper joint tape
Sandpaper (medium grade)

 **SAFETY TIPS**

Protect your eyes with goggles when hammering or using power tools.

Anatomy of a wall.
This short dividing wall is just long enough to hide the toilet. Built of 2-by-4 studs fastened between a soleplate and a top plate, the wall is secured to an existing wall stud as well as to the floor and ceiling joists, or to blocking installed between these members. Sheets of wallboard are fastened to the framing with adhesive and screws.

TOP PLATE

CEILING JOISTS

STUDS

EXISTING STUD

FLOOR JOISTS

WALLBOARD

SOLEPLATE

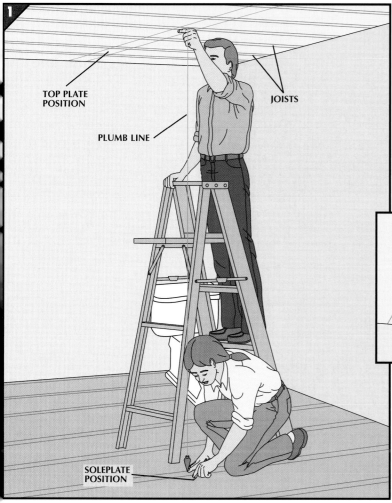

TOP PLATE POSITION

JOISTS

PLUMB LINE

SOLEPLATE POSITION

1. Planning the location.

◆ With an electronic stud finder, locate the ceiling joists and mark their positions. If the joists run parallel to the planned wall, situate the wall to fall directly under a joist. If you cannot place the wall under a joist, open the ceiling between the joists on each side of the planned location and install nailer blocks with joist hangers (inset).

◆ Snap two chalk lines on the ceiling that represent the position of the wall's top plate.

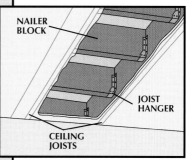

NAILER BLOCK

JOIST HANGER

CEILING JOISTS

◆ With a plumb bob, transfer the location of the top plate to the floor (left), then snap two more chalk lines for the soleplate.

◆ If the soleplate runs perpendicular to the floor joists, mark their locations. When the joists run parallel to the soleplate and the flooring material is less than $1\frac{1}{8}$ inches thick, add nailing blocks between the floor joists as you did at the ceiling.

> ⚠ **CAUTION** *Before cutting into the ceiling or floor, check for the presence of lead and asbestos* (page 43).

2. Marking the plates.

◆ From 2-by-4 framing lumber, cut a soleplate and top plate the length of the new wall, then lay them on-edge side by side and drive a nail partway through them to hold them together.

◆ Beginning at one end, mark the plates every 16 inches to indicate the stud locations (right). Plan for studs at both ends of the wall, making the space between studs at one end narrower if necessary.

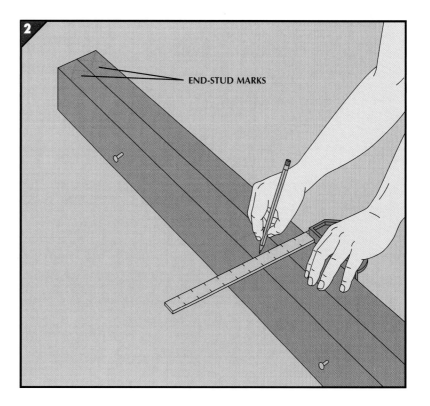

END-STUD MARKS

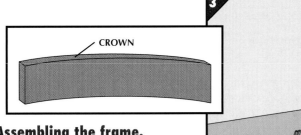

CROWN

3. Assembling the frame.

◆ Every 2 feet along a soleplate line, measure the distance from the ceiling to the floor. Cut 2-by-4 studs $3\frac{1}{4}$ inches shorter than the smallest measurement.
◆ With $3\frac{1}{2}$-inch nails, fasten the studs to the plates at the marked positions *(right)*, making sure that any crowned boards are placed face up *(inset)*.

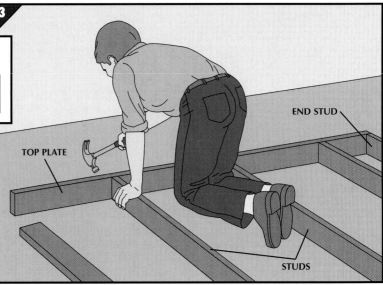

TOP PLATE

END STUD

STUDS

STUD

4. Raising the wall.

◆ Locate the studs in the existing wall.
◆ With a helper, raise the new wall into position. If the wall lines up with a stud in the adjacent wall, attach the end stud with 3-inch wallboard screws every 24 inches *(left)*; otherwise, secure the end stud to nailer blocks installed in the adjacent wall as you would for the ceiling *(page 61, Step 1)*.
◆ Push paired cedar shims, one from each side, between the top plate and the ceiling. Place them every 16 inches along a parallel joist, or at the location of every perpendicular joist or nailer block.
◆ Drive screws through the top plate and shims into the joist, joists, or nailer blocks. Score protruding shims with a utility knife and snap them off.
◆ Drive screws through the soleplate into each perpendicular joist or nailer block, or at 16-inch intervals into a parallel joist.

A HALF-HEIGHT WALL
. . . .

A half-height wall is a good choice for dividing a room with only one light source. It also offers space on the top for a narrow shelf. If you want a wider top shelf, build the wall with 2-by-6s instead of 2-by-4s. Assemble the outer frame as you would a regular wall, then cut a cross member to fit between the end studs and nail it at the desired height. Cut cripple studs and install them at 16-inch intervals between the cross member and the soleplate.

CROSS MEMBER

CRIPPLE STUDS

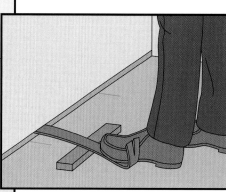

Putting up panels.

◆ Mark the stud centers on the ceiling and floor, and trim the first panel to the length of the wall or to end at the center of a stud.

◆ With a caulking gun, run a $\frac{3}{8}$-inch-thick bead of wallboard adhesive along the studs, starting and stopping several inches from where the edges of panels will fall to prevent adhesive from squeezing out between them.

◆ With a helper, lift the first panel into place against the ceiling *(above)*.

◆ Fit an electric drill with a dimpler, then drive $1\frac{1}{2}$-inch wallboard screws through the panel into studs 1 inch from the bottom, across the middle, and 1 inch from the top. At the ends, space screws every 8 inches, $\frac{1}{2}$ inch from the edge. For a long wall, butt a second panel end-to-end with the first.

◆ Once the top half of the wall is covered, install the lower panels trimmed lengthwise to leave a $\frac{1}{2}$-inch gap at the floor; lift the panels with a foot lever *(inset)* to fasten them. If more than one panel is required, stagger the end joints in the courses.

◆ Hang panels on the other side of the wall in the same manner.

◆ For the end of the wall, cut pieces equal to the stud width plus the wallboard thickness on each side of the wall. Apply adhesive to the stud and screw the pieces to it every 16 inches.

Follow the same technique to install panels vertically, but trim them to the height of the wall less $\frac{1}{2}$ inch.

Protecting the outside corners.

◆ With tin snips, trim a strip of metal corner bead to the height of the wall, cutting through one flange at a time.

◆ Position the corner bead over a wallboard joint at the end of the wall and drive screws at every sixth hole into the stud.

◆ Cover the other joint at the end of the wall in the same way *(right)*.

END OF WALL

CORNER BEAD

CONCEALING FASTENERS AND SEAMS

1. Filling the screwheads.
◆ Load half the width of a 5-inch taping knife with joint compound.
◆ Holding the blade almost parallel to the wallboard, draw the knife across the screwhead, filling the dimple completely with compound *(left)*.
◆ Turn the blade at a right angle to the first stroke and scrape off the excess compound.
◆ Apply two additional coats in the same way, allowing the compound to dry between applications
◆ Once the third coat dries, smooth the surface with medium-grade sandpaper or a damp wallboard sponge.

2. Covering seams.
Load half the width of a 5-inch taping knife with joint compound, then run it smoothly along the joint to fill the depression formed by the tapered edges of the panels. Center the blade over the joint, then angle it gradually closer to the wallboard as you draw it along the seam *(right)*.

For end-to-end joints, where the panels do not have tapered edges, apply a $\frac{1}{8}$-inch-thick layer of compound.

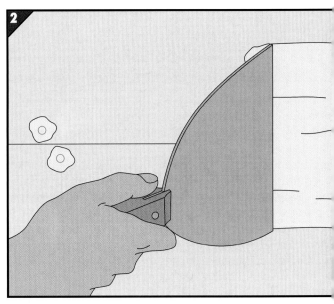

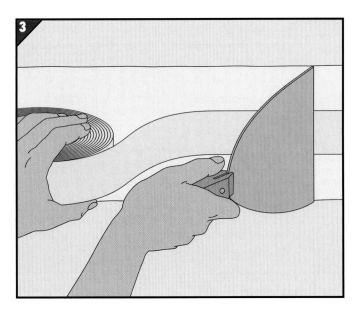

3. Taping the seams.
◆ Press the end of a roll of paper joint tape into the wet compound spread along the joint.
◆ Unroll the tape over the joint, then run the blade over it to force it into the compound *(left)* Using the knife as a straightedge, tear the tape at the end of the joint.
◆ Make a second and third pass with the knife to scrape off the excess compound and eliminate any air bubbles.

At end-to-end joints, leave a combined tape-and compound thickness of about $\frac{1}{8}$ inch.

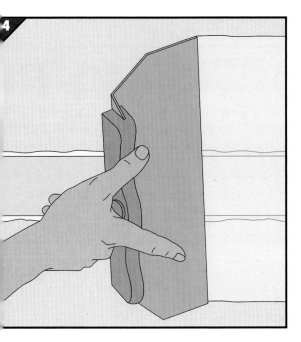

4. Feathering the seams.

◆ With the full width of a 10-inch knife, cover the joint tape with an even layer of the compound (left).

◆ Clean the knife and draw it over the compound, holding the blade slightly off center and lifting the edge nearest the joint about $\frac{1}{8}$ inch. Make a similar pass on the other side of the joint to create a slight ridge in the center that feathers out evenly on both sides.

◆ Let the compound dry, then lightly sand or sponge it smooth.

◆ Apply a final layer of compound with two passes of the knife. On the first pass, rest one end of the blade on the ridge of dried compound and bear down on the other end; on the second pass, repeat the procedure on the other side of the ridge.

◆ Once the compound dries, give it a final sanding or sponging.

For end-to-end joints, feather the compound 20 inches on either side of the joint.

FINISHING CORNERS

Outside corners.

◆ Load the left side of a 5-inch knife with joint compound, and draw it slowly down the left side of the corner bead, allowing the right side of the blade to overhang (right).

◆ Load the right side of the knife and run it down the right side of the bead.

◆ Clean the knife, then run it down both faces of the bead, smoothing the joint and removing excess compound.

◆ Apply and smooth a second coat, this time without letting the knife overhang the corner; feather this layer about $1\frac{1}{2}$ inches beyond the first.

◆ With an 8-inch knife, apply a third coat of compound and feather it an additional 2 inches on each side.

◆ After the compound dries, sand or sponge it smooth.

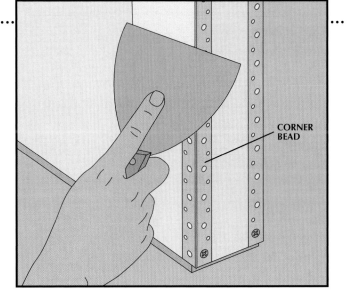

CORNER BEAD

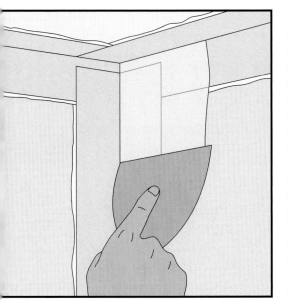

Covering inside corners.

◆ Apply joint compound with a 5-inch taping knife, running the blade along one side of the corner and then the other, lifting the inside edge slightly to provide a thicker layer of compound at the joint.

◆ Crease joint tape along its center fold and press it lightly into the compound. Run the knife over the tape, pressing hard enough to smooth it and squeeze out excess compound.

◆ Apply an even layer of compound along one side of the corner (left). Scrape off any compound that laps onto the second side of the corner, then draw the knife along the first side again, bearing down on the blade's outside edge to feather the compound. Make another pass to smooth this layer, removing excess and scraping off compound left on the wall beyond the feathered edge.

◆ Let the compound dry, then feather the other side of the corner in the same way.

◆ Repeat the feathering procedure on both sides of the corner with an 8-inch knife.

The Master Bath

A few special additions can transform a master bath into a private retreat. Rela in a platform tub or whirlpool, or unwind in a steam bath installed in place of a ordinary shower stall. Put in a customized lighting scheme, or add a glass-bloc window to provide natural light without sacrificing privacy. Treat your toes to con fort by installing a radiant-heat floor that stays warm in winter.

Tiling a raised-tub platform →

The Master Bath: A Private Retreat

For many people, a master bath is a personal haven where they can become quickly energized in the morning or unwind leisurely at day's end. To get the most from your master bath, you can plan alterations that will save you time as well as let you pamper yourself.

When deciding on what changes to make, look first at your bathing preferences. Are you someone who relishes a lengthy soak in the tub, or are you more inclined to value a quick jump into and out of the shower? Once you have made the basic choice of tub or shower—or a combination of the two—you can begin to plan the other features of the room to integrate them with the fixture.

Space constraints may restrict some of your choices, but probably not to a great extent. The range of plumbing fixtures, amenities, and accessories available on the market is astounding. Bathtubs and showers are made in many different sizes and shapes—large, small, and in-between; round,

A stepped glass-block window makes a dramatic backdrop to a platform tub, providing natural light without sacrificing privacy. The half-height divider enhances the cozy feel of the fixture, and carries out the design theme in its single row of glass blocks. Shelving recessed into the wall puts towels and other amenities within reach.

Natural sunlight from a window and a skylight floods this bathroom during the day. A strip of incandescent bulbs provides controlled light for the vanity area. The tub gives the illusion of being sunken, but is actually set in a stepped platform.

oval, and rectangular. There are even hourglass-shaped tubs for two. You can also find square and triangular units that fit neatly into a corner, practical for rooms with a limited amount of space. And don't overlook the comfort and charm of antique fixtures. An old-fashioned claw-foot tub may be just the right thing to suit your needs and tastes.

Fixtures are also available with special features that make them particularly appropriate for a luxurious master bath.

Whirlpool tubs with pulsating jets of water will massage and relax tired muscles *(page 95)*. A combination steam-bath/shower *(pages 96-109)* can afford a rejuvenating pick-up after a strenuous exercise session.

When considering what kinds of lighting fixtures to install, plan a scheme that is versatile. In general, a lighting system should provide adequate illumination for specific activities, but not conflict with the mood you want to create. Task areas

Even in a bathroom of modest proportions, you can still build in luxury by installing a freestanding corner whirlpool tub.

taining privacy. The blocks create a shimmering wall that can brighten up the whole room and make a delightful focal point. You may want to consider installing a skylight, which admits up to five times as much light as a window of the same size. Just a two-foot square skylight can illuminate a room well enough that you can forego electrical lighting during the day.

Colors can be powerful mood setters. You can cool the visual "temperature" of the room with blues and greens, or generate a warm, bright atmosphere with reds, yellows, and oranges. Or, create a calming sanctuary by applying light, neutral tones and subdued tints. Sponged paint, shiny

such as the vanity, bathtub, and shower need to be well-lighted. For these and other spots that are regularly exposed to water, recessed ceiling fixtures are a good choice. Dimmer switches *(pages 72)* controlling small spotlights on interesting focal points such as potted plants or artwork, for instance, can add tremendously to the relaxing ambiance of the room. Indirect lighting is especially effective when you want to create a soft glow *(pages 73-75)*. Low-voltage strip lights mounted in the steps leading to a platform tub can accentuate the area as well as be a deterrent to accidents.

Windows are practical additions to a master bath, enlarging the sense of space and providing light. A window built of glass blocks *(pages 76-83)* is a particularly good way to bring in natural light while main-

A combination steam bath and shower provides a place to really relax, but it takes up no more space than a typical shower stall.

Recessed lighting above the vanity brightly illuminates this task area, while a soft, indirect glow cascades from hidden ceiling fixtures.

glass, natural tile, or rough-hewn wood paneling all lend themselves well to the subtle contrast of pale hues.

In choosing flooring materials, keep the visual-interest theme in mind. Ceramic tiles are a favorite, but natural stone is an interesting alternative. Granite and slate are available in dark gray or green, sometimes with hints of pink; the random pattern and subtle variations of the material can provide just the textured effect you want. You might decide as well to treat bare feet to a bit of luxury by installing radiant-heating cables before you lay down the finish material *(pages 110-117).* This self-contained heating system will maintain the floor at a uniform, constant temperature, even on a cold winter morning.

If space allows, you can venture beyond simple notions of bathroom and build in other features. Including an exercise corner, a sound system, or a chaise and a shelf of books will make the room even more a personal retreat.

Dimmer switches and indirect lighting can be used to create dramatic effects in a master bath. A dimmer switch has a knob or toggle that adjusts the level of light from low to high, allowing you to control the brightness. When the main fixture is not needed, you can use indirect lighting for a softer glow.

Dimmer Switches: A bathroom light is generally controlled at one location, and requires a two-way, or single-pole, dimmer rather than a three-way type. Instead of screw terminals, a single-pole dimmer has two lead wires, which may be black or red. Most codes require that the switch also have a green ground wire, which is joined to the bare copper wires of the electrical cable and a jumper with a wire cap; the jumper is attached at the other end to the ground screw in the electrical box. If the dimmer is to control a fluorescent fixture, you will need a model specifically designed for fluorescents.

Indirect Lighting: A channel near the top of a wall directs light upward, reflecting it off the ceiling in a gentle glow *(pages 73-75)*. The channel can be made of ordinary wood and painted to match the walls or ceilings, and the inside surfaces painted glossy white to maximize light distribution. This setup requires fluorescent tubes, since incandescent bulbs generate too much heat and can be a fire hazard in this confined space.

To bring power to the fixture, run a new circuit from the service panel *(pages 121-122)* to a switch for the circuit near the bathroom door. Have a licensed electrician check your work and connect the circuit at the service panel.

⚠ **CAUTION** *Before working on an existing circuit, turn off the power at the service panel and check that it is off (pages 119-120). If the house has aluminum wiring, follow the precautions on page 119.*

 TOOLS

Screwdriver	Circular saw or table saw
Electric drill	Handscrew
Stud finder	clamps
Chalk line	Cable ripper
Carpenter's level	Electrician's
Fish tape	multipurpose tool

 **MATERIALS** Electrical box

	Wall switch
Dimmer switch	Wire caps
Fluorescent	5/4 x 6 lumber
fixtures and	Wood screws
tubes	($\frac{1}{2}$" No. 6,
Electrical cable	1$\frac{3}{4}$" No. 8,
Jumper wires	2$\frac{1}{2}$" No. 10)

SAFETY TIPS

Protect your eyes with goggles when drilling or using a power saw.

ADDING A DIMMER SWITCH

Hooking up a two-way dimmer switch.
◆ Turn off electricity to the circuit *(page 119)*, then unscrew the cover plate of the wall switch and check that the power is off *(page 120)*.
◆ Disconnect the old switch and set it aside.
◆ Prepare the wires and connect them with caps *(pages 121-122)*: For a metal box that has more than one cable, join the black wires to one of the dimmer switch's black leads and the white wires to the switch's other black lead. Join the cables' bare copper wires, the switch's green ground wire, and a jumper with a wire cap, then attach the other end of the jumper to the box's ground screw *(right)*. If the box is plastic, omit the jumper.

When only one cable enters the box, join the black, white, and ground wires in the same way, but recode the cable's white wire as black with a piece of electrical tape *(inset)*.

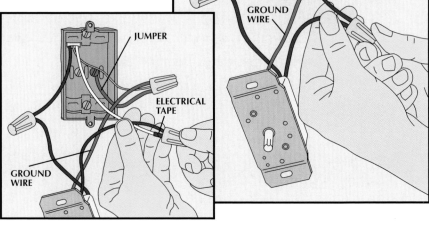

1. Wiring the new circuit.

◆ Drill a hole 3 inches from the corner and 16 inches below the ceiling in the wall adjoining the one on which the light channel will be installed.

◆ Run a cable from the service panel to the location for the switch and another cable from there to the drilled hole, install a box for the switch and clamp the cables in it, and prepare the cable and switch wires (pages 120-122).

◆ Attach the black wire of one cable to the switch's brass terminal and the black wire of the other cable to the switch's silver terminal.

◆ Join the cables' white wires with a wire cap.

◆ Cap together the cables' bare copper wires, the switch's green wire, and a jumper, then fasten the jumper to the box's grounding screw (right)—omit the jumper if the box is plastic.

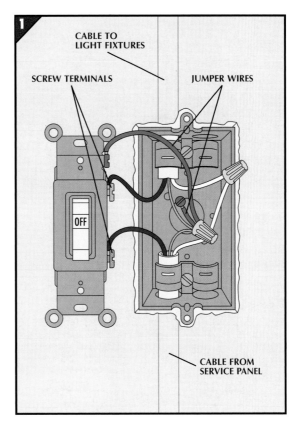

2. Assembling the channel.

◆ Cut two 5/4-by-6 boards to the length of the wall.

◆ Prop one of the boards on edge, supporting it with handscrew clamps, then set the second board on top of it and drill countersunk pilot holes for $1\frac{3}{4}$-inch No. 8 screws every 16 inches.

◆ Drive the screws (left).

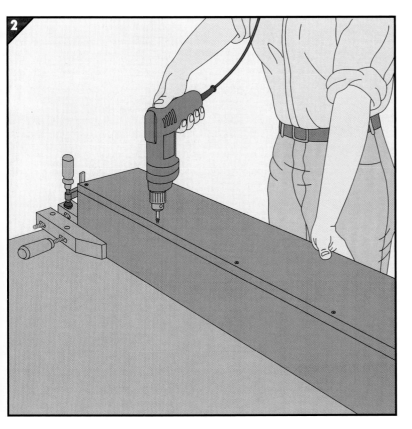

3. Installing the channel.

◆ Snap a level chalk line along the wall 12 inches below the ceiling.

◆ With an electronic stud finder, mark the stud locations along the line.

◆ Have a helper hold the channel so the joint between the boards faces down and the top is aligned with the chalk line, then drill pilot holes for two $2\frac{1}{2}$-inch No. 10 screws at each stud location and drive the screws *(right)*.

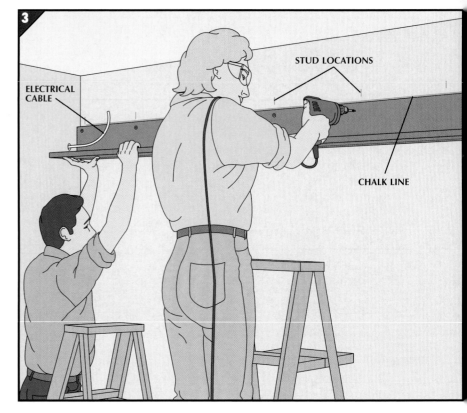

4. Positioning the fixtures.

◆ Remove the knockouts from the ends of the light-fixture housings.

◆ Set the housings on the bottom of the channel at least $\frac{1}{2}$ inch away from the front edges, staggering them to fit if necessary. Fasten them down with $\frac{1}{2}$-inch No. 6 screws *(left)*.

◆ Run the incoming cable through the clamp of a two-part connector *(page 122)*, then feed the cable through the knockout in the first housing and put the connector's nut over the cable.

◆ Route a second cable, long enough to reach the second light fixture, out through the nut and clamp, then clamp the cables in the knockout.

◆ Feed the second cable into the next fixture *(inset)*, then run cable to each additional fixture in the same manner.

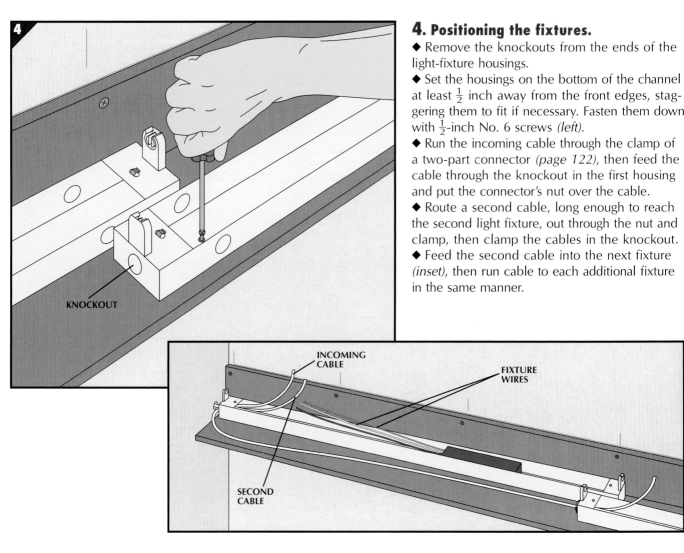

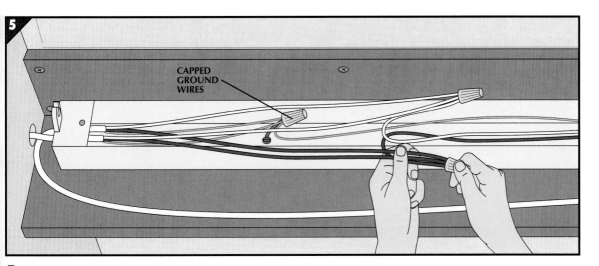

CAPPED GROUND WIRES

5. Wiring the fixtures.

◆ Cut back the sheathing on the cables and strip the ends of the wires *(page 121)*.

◆ Attach a short green jumper wire to the ground screw in the first fixture and join it with a wire cap *(page 122)* to the bare-copper ground wires of the fixture and the two cables.

◆ Cap the like-colored wires of the cables and fixture: white to white and black to black *(above)*.

◆ Wire the remaining fixtures in the same way.

6. Installing the covers and tubes.

◆ Tuck all the wires into the fixture housings, then snap the covers into place.

◆ Install the lighting tubes by orienting their end pins vertically and fitting them into the socket slots *(right)*, then turn the tubes until they lock into position.

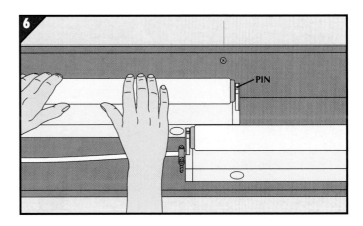

PIN

7. Fastening the front.

◆ Cut a 5/4-by-6 board to the same length as the others.

◆ Have a helper hold the front piece in position flush with the bottom of the channel.

◆ Drill pilot holes for $1\frac{3}{4}$-inch No. 8 screws through the front piece into the bottom, spacing the holes every 16 inches, then drive the screws *(left)*.

A Glass-Block Wall

Natural light brightens up any bathroom. A glass-block window in an exterior wall lets in sunshine but maintains privacy.

Choosing the Blocks: Glass blocks come in standard squares of 6, 8, and 12 inches—these sizes include an allowance for a $\frac{1}{4}$-inch mortar joint between units. The blocks are available in a range of patterns, some more opaque than others. Special types of blocks with a higher R-value provide greater insulation in an exterior wall. All varieties are set in white mortar intended for use with glass-block units.

Framing the Opening: Glass blocks cannot directly support the weight of the structure above them. To insert a panel of blocks into an exterior wall, you will need to frame the opening *(pages 77-79)*—make it an even multiple of the 6, 8, or 12 inches, plus $\frac{1}{2}$ inch horizontally and vertically for expansion strips. The opening can extend to the floor or stop at a sill plate installed at the desired height.

Bearing and Nonbearing Walls: Walls that run perpendicular to ceiling joists generally support the weight of the house framing and are referred to as bearing walls. Before cutting into a bearing wall, you must temporarily shore up the joists with a support wall *(opposite, Step 1)*. Walls that run parallel to the joists are typically nonbearing and do not require a support wall.

 CAUTION *Before cutting into wall materials, check for the presence of lead and asbestos (page 43).*

 TOOLS

Circular saw	Rubber mallet
Wallboard saw	Carpenter's
Wood chisel	nippers
Electric drill	Tin snips
Chalk line	Pliers
Combination	Staple gun
square	Plastic tub
Plumb bob	Mason's trowel
Carpenter's level	Striking tool
Pry bar	Sponge
Hammer	Caulking gun

MATERIALS

1 x 4, 2 x 4s	Expansion strips	Finishing nails (2")
LVL boards or	Panel anchors	Wood screws
header stock	Plastic spacers	($1\frac{1}{2}$" No. 8)
Shims	Reinforcing wire	White mortar
Trim and casing	Common nails	Silicone caulk
Glass blocks	($2\frac{1}{2}$", 3", $3\frac{1}{2}$")	Grout sealer

 **SAFETY TIPS**

Wear safety goggles when hammering or using power tools, and add a dust mask before tearing out wall materials. Put on gloves to work with mortar.

Anatomy of a glass-block wall.

The opening for this glass-block window is framed with a jack stud and king stud on each side, a header at the top, and a sill at the bottom. Cripple studs fill in above the header and below the sill.

The blocks are laid in courses with plastic spacers and mortar between all the units. Once the installation is complete, the tabs on the spacers are snapped off and the holes filled with mortar. Expansion strips are placed at the perimeter of the opening. Panel anchors tie courses of blocks to the framing—every second course for 6- or 8-inch blocks, every course for 12-inch blocks. For panels bigger than 25 square feet, reinforcing wire is added every second course.

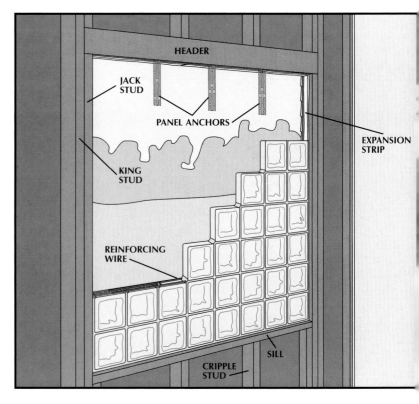

FRAMING THE OPENING

1. Building a support wall.

When the floor and ceiling joists run perpendicular to the wall, build a temporary support wall before you cut the opening.

◆ Cut two 2-by-4 top plates and soleplates 4 feet longer than the planned width of the opening and fasten the double plates together with $2\frac{1}{2}$ inch common nails.

◆ Measure the distance between the floor and the ceiling, then cut studs $6\frac{1}{4}$ inches shorter than this measurement.

◆ Assemble the support wall as described on pages 61 to 62, then raise it in place, positioning it about 4 feet from the wall.

◆ Attach a 1-by-4 brace diagonally across the support wall from the floor to the ceiling, nailing it to each stud.

◆ Drive shims between the double top plate and the ceiling at the joist locations, shimming until the structure fits tightly (right). Recheck for plumb as you work.

If there is a basement or crawlspace beneath the temporary wall, support the floor joists with a horizontal 4-by-6 beam held up with 4-by-4 posts. For an opening in a second-story wall, erect a supporting framework on both the first and second floors.

2. Cutting the studs.

◆ Turn off the power to any circuits that pass through the wall to be opened (page 119).

◆ Outline the planned opening and mark the stud locations within the outline. With a wallboard saw, cut away the wallboard from the floor to the ceiling between the nearest studs on each side of the opening.

◆ With a circular saw, make two cuts a few inches apart in the middle of each stud within the planned opening (left), then knock out the small pieces and complete the cuts with a wood chisel—or, saw all the way through the studs with a reciprocating saw.

◆ Pry the studs away from the sheathing with a pry bar.

◆ Cut nails protruding from the top plate, soleplate, and sheathing with carpenter's nippers.

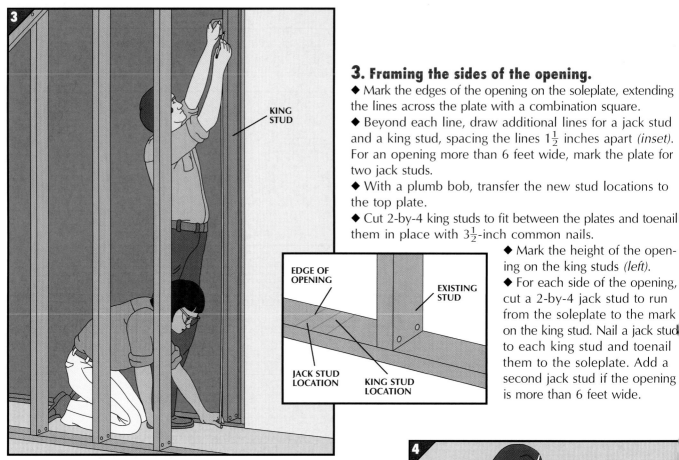

KING STUD

EDGE OF OPENING

EXISTING STUD

JACK STUD LOCATION

KING STUD LOCATION

3. Framing the sides of the opening.

◆ Mark the edges of the opening on the soleplate, extending the lines across the plate with a combination square.

◆ Beyond each line, draw additional lines for a jack stud and a king stud, spacing the lines $1\frac{1}{2}$ inches apart *(inset)*. For an opening more than 6 feet wide, mark the plate for two jack studs.

◆ With a plumb bob, transfer the new stud locations to the top plate.

◆ Cut 2-by-4 king studs to fit between the plates and toenail them in place with $3\frac{1}{2}$-inch common nails.

◆ Mark the height of the opening on the king studs *(left)*.

◆ For each side of the opening, cut a 2-by-4 jack stud to run from the soleplate to the mark on the king stud. Nail a jack stud to each king stud and toenail them to the soleplate. Add a second jack stud if the opening is more than 6 feet wide.

4. Constructing a header.

◆ Consult the chart below to determine the size of lumber required for the header, according to the span and the load above the opening. When the header will reach almost to the top plate, consider making it wide enough to meet the top plate to avoid having to add cripple studs above it.

◆ For a header made of lumber, cut two pieces of wood and one piece of $\frac{1}{2}$-inch plywood to the distance between the king studs, and fasten the pieces together, staggering $3\frac{1}{2}$-inch common nails at 10-inch intervals *(right)*. If the header will be made of laminated-veneer lumber (LVL), nail together two pieces of $1\frac{3}{4}$-inch LVL with no plywood between them.

PLYWOOD

CHOOSING THE RIGHT HEADER

Load above opening	Span				
	4'	6'	8'	10'	12'
Roof only	2 x 4	2 x 6	2 x 8	2 x 10	2 x 12
One story	2 x 6	2 x 8	2 x 10	2 x 12	—
Two stories	2 x 10	2 x 10	2 x 12	—	—

Matching a header to load and span.

To find the dimensions of lumber for a header, match the span of the opening with the load above it. For a span that falls between those listed, use the column for the next larger span. When the entry for the span and load is blank, buy an LVL header; take the information on span and load to the dealer to determine the correct size of LVL for the opening.

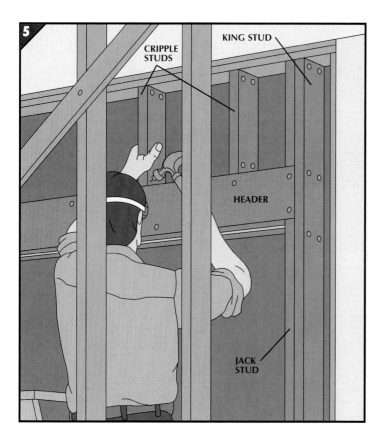

5. Framing the top.

◆ With a helper, lift the header into place between the king studs and rest it on the jack studs.

◆ Nail through the king studs into the ends of the header, then toenail the jack studs to the bottom of the header.

◆ Cut 2-by-4 cripple studs to fit between the header and the top plate, and nail a cripple stud to each king stud.

◆ Toenail additional cripple studs every 16 inches to the header and top plate *(left)*.

6. Framing the bottom.

◆ Mark the height of the bottom of the opening on the jack studs. Add marks $1\frac{1}{2}$ inches below the first ones for the bottom of the sill.

◆ Cut two cripple studs to fit from the top of the soleplate to the bottom marks. Nail a cripple to each jack stud, then toenail them to the soleplate.

◆ Cut a 2-by-4 sill to fit between the jack studs and set it in place on top of the cripple studs. Nail the sill to each cripple stud *(right)* and toenail it to the jack studs.

◆ Fit additional cripple studs between the sill and soleplate every 16 inches and toenail them in place.

For an opening that will extend to the floor, cut a 2-by-4 to fit between the jack studs and nail it to the soleplate to create a 3-inch-high curb.

1. Marking the opening.
◆ From inside the house, drill a hole at each corner of the opening, using a drill bit extension if necessary.
◆ Draw lines connecting the holes using a straight board as a guide *(right)*.

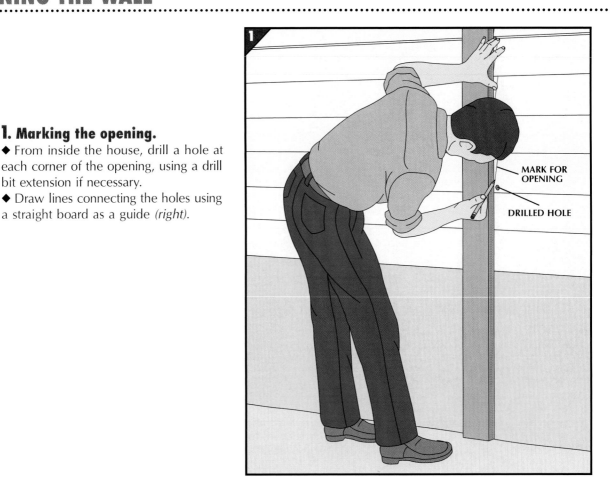

MARK FOR OPENING

DRILLED HOLE

2. Cutting the opening.
◆ Cut through the siding and sheathing along the lines with a circular saw *(left)* (for aluminum siding, use a metal-cutting blade). For vertical cuts on overlapping siding, create a flat surface for the saw's baseplate by tacking a 1-by-4 to the siding. Finish the cuts at the corners with a wood chisel, tin snips for aluminum.
◆ Remove the cut siding and sheathing from the wall, using a pry bar if necessary.
◆ Mark the siding $2\frac{3}{4}$ inches outside the opening. Set the blade of the circular saw to the depth of the siding only and cut back the siding to accommodate the trim *(page 83, Step 8)*.

LAYING THE BLOCKS

1. Adding anchors and expansion strips.

◆ For 6- or 12-inch blocks, mark the jack studs and header at intervals of 12 inches—for 8-inch blocks, every 16 inches.

◆ Cut panel anchors 12 inches long with tin snips and bend them 3 inches from one end. With two $1\frac{1}{2}$-inch No. 8 wood screws, fasten the short leg of an anchor at each line.

◆ Cut lengths of expansion strip to fit along the sides of the opening between anchors, covering their short arms. Trim the strips to a width of $2\frac{1}{4}$ inches.

◆ Staple the expansion strips between each pair of anchors (right).

2. Preparing the spacers.

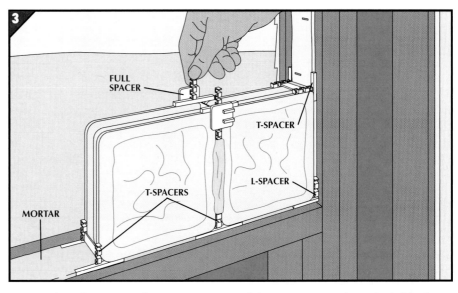

L-spacers are placed in each corner of the panel, while T-spacers are set between the perimeter blocks. Full spacers are used elsewhere.

◆ To make L-spacers, snip off one tab with pliers, turn the spacer on its end on the remaining tab, then snip off one half of one base (left) and one half of one cross leg. Flip the spacer over and remove the corresponding half of the other base and cross leg, as well as the other tab.

◆ For T-spacers, remove both tabs and half of each cross leg.

3. Laying the first course.

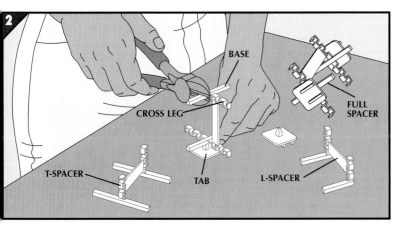

◆ Pour mortar mix into a plastic tub, add water, and blend until the mortar is the consistency of bread dough, but not crumbly. Mix only as much as you think you can use in 30 minutes.

◆ With a mason's trowel, spread a $\frac{1}{4}$-inch bed of mortar on the sill.

◆ Set a block into the mortar at one end of the sill, placing an L-spacer in the bottom corner against the expansion strip, a T-spacer under the other bottom corner, and a T-spacer at the top corner against the expansion strip.

◆ Spread a $\frac{1}{2}$-inch layer of mortar on one edge of a second block and set it in place, slipping another T-spacer under the exposed corner; add a full spacer on top of the two blocks with the crossbar down (right).

◆ Complete the row in the same way, laying the last block with an L-spacer in the bottom corner.

◆ Place a long carpenter's level on top of the course; tap down high blocks with a rubber mallet.

◆ With a damp sponge, smooth any extruded mortar back into the joints.

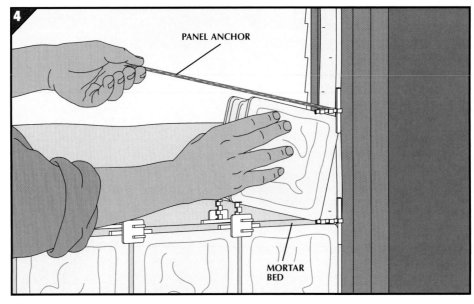

4. Setting the second course.

◆ Spread mortar across the top of the first course, keeping the spacer bases as mortar-free as possible.

◆ Lift the anchor to fit the first couple of blocks in place *(above)*.

◆ Lay the rest of the blocks in the course as for the first one.

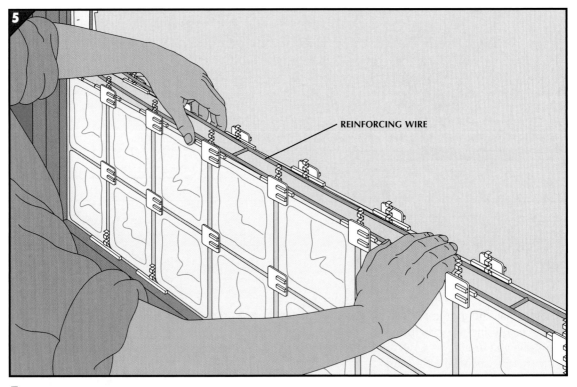

5. Adding reinforcement.

◆ Once the second course is complete, spread a bed of mortar over the top of the blocks, covering the panel anchors.

◆ With tin snips, cut reinforcing wire to fit across the course; plan an overlap of 6 inches when more than one length is needed. Set the wire into the mortar *(above)*.

◆ Continue building the wall, laying reinforcing wire every second course of blocks. After completing every few courses, check the wall for plumb with a carpenter's level and tap any protruding blocks into place with a rubber mallet.

◆ As you reach the header at the top of the opening, fit the vertical panel anchors into place between the blocks.

6. Putting in the top course.

◆ With pliers, snap the tabs off the spacers on top of the second-to-last course.
◆ Fit an L-spacer on the top corner of a glass block, then angle the block into place in the corner. Fit a T-spacer into place at the exposed corner of the block.
◆ Angle a second block into place *(right)* and add a T-spacer.
◆ Complete the top course in the same way, fitting the last block into place with an L-spacer in the corner.

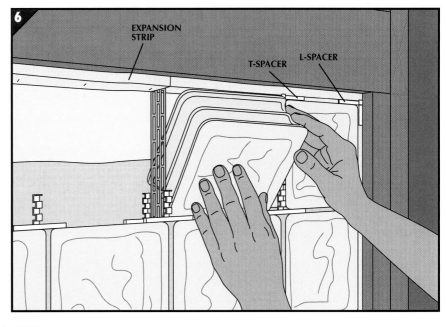

7. Finishing the joints.

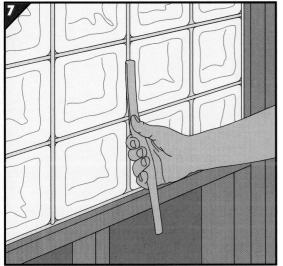

◆ With pliers, twist the spacer tabs off both sides of the wall.
◆ Fill any holes and gaps in the joints with mortar, then wipe excess mortar off the blocks with a damp sponge or cloth.
◆ Let the mortar set for one to two hours, or until it is stiff enough to hold a thumbprint.
◆ With a convex striking tool, smooth the horizontal mortar joints, then smooth the vertical joints *(left)*.
◆ Wait one to two hours, then wipe the block faces with a soft, clean cloth to remove any film.
◆ Run a bead of silicone caulk along the edges of the wall.

8. Adding trim.

◆ Cut 1-by-4 cedar or pressure-treated boards long enough to cover the edges of the cut siding on the outside of the house; miter the ends of the boards.
◆ Fit a length of trim into place on the sheathing, butting it against the siding. Nail the trim to the sheathing with 2-inch finishing nails every 16 inches. Install the remaining pieces of trim in the same way *(right)*.
◆ Measure the distance between the trim and glass blocks, and cut strips of 1-by molding stock to fit the gap. Fit the strips into place and nail through the trim into them.
◆ Apply a bead of silicone caulk where the trim meets the glass blocks and where it meets the siding.
◆ Inside, patch the wallboard to cover the framing, then install window casing and a filler strip in the same way as on the exterior. Caulk between the blocks and the trim.
◆ When the mortar joints have set for one week, brush on a clear silicone or acrylic grout sealer.

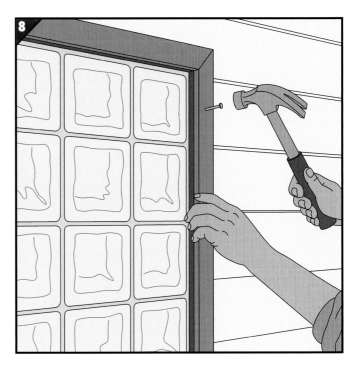

Installing a Platform Tub

Inviting and luxurious, a platform tub is a sumptuous addition to a master bath. Such a platform can also accommodate a whirlpool bath.

Situating the Tub: Platform tubs are generally deeper and wider than standard tubs. Since they typically do not incorporate a shower, they need no end wall for the plumbing and can be located almost anywhere in the room. Refer to pages 123 to 125 for basic plumbing techniques, tools, and materials.

The tub on these pages replaces a standard model situated in an alcove. The end wall containing the plumbing is removed, and the supply and drain lines are extended a short distance. When the tub has only one end wall, the job will be easier: Simply remove the old bathtub and construct the platform to the desired length. If the existing tub fills the space between two walls, your options will be limited since you must select a tub that is the same length as the existing one. You can also place a tub in the middle of a bathroom by building a four-sided platform.

Building the Platform: The ledges of the platform need not be the same width all around, but the one against an existing wall should be no more than 8 inches wide to be adequately supported. To avoid having to cut large numbers of tiles, size the ledges to accommodate whole tiles.

Walls and Floor: To remove the old tub, you will need to strip off a section of wall tile around it. If you can match the existing tile, patch the surface; or, cut away the tile and wallboard and install water-resistant wallboard. When you remove flooring to fit the platform, trim it along the outline of the platform. If this is difficult to do neatly, cut it back further and patch it before tiling the platform walls.

 CAUTION *Before tearing out wall or flooring materials, check for the presence of lead and asbestos (page 43).*

TOOLS

Pipe wrench
Adjustable wrench
Channel-joint pliers
Cold chisel
Ball-peen hammer
Screwdriver
Hammer
Chalk line
Carpenter's level
Stud finder
Circular saw
Saber saw
Hacksaw
Electric drill
Tile cutter
Tile nippers
Notched trowel
Grout float
Caulking gun

MATERIALS

Tub
1 x 2s, 2 x 4s
Exterior plywood ($\frac{3}{4}$")
Shims
Drainpipe and fittings
Supply pipe and fittings
Faucets and spout
Overflow-and-drain kit
Flexible supply tubes
Common nails ($1\frac{1}{4}$", 3")
Screws ($1\frac{1}{2}$" No. 8) and
  cup washers
Tiles
Premixed mortar
Latex-modified thinset
  mortar and tile grout
Silicone caulk
Grout sealer

SAFETY TIPS

Protect your eyes with goggles when using hammers, power tools, and propane torches.

Anatomy of a platform tub.

This tub sits in a plywood platform supported by two low stud walls and cleats fastened to the existing walls. The platform's ledges and walls are tiled, and it incorporates a removable end panel *(not shown)* for access to the plumbing. A skirtless tub fits into a cutout in the plywood top, and rests on a mortar bed on the subfloor. The hot- and cold-water supply pipes are fitted with shutoff valves, and flexible supply tubes extend from the valves to the deck-mounted faucets. A special drain-overflow pipe connects to the drainpipe in the floor.

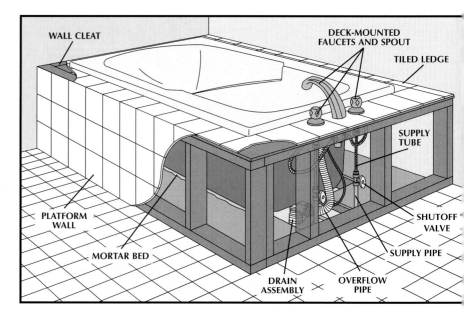

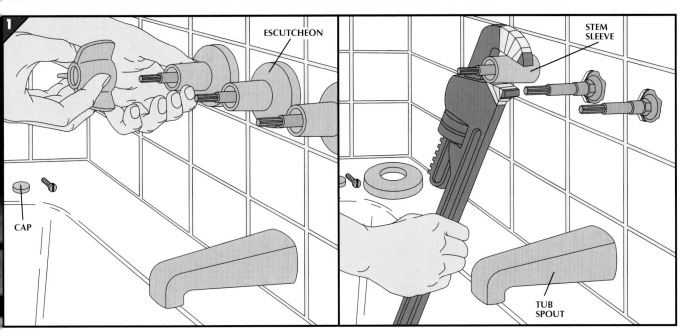

1. Taking off the faucets.

If the tub has a single-handle faucet, use the techniques on page 54 to remove it. For a double-handle model, turn off the water supply to the tub and drain the pipes *(page 124)*.

◆ Pry off or unscrew the caps in the faucet handles.

◆ Remove the screw holding each handle, then pull the handles from the faucet stems *(above, left)*.

◆ If the escutcheons have setscrews or face screws, loosen them, then pry the escutcheons from the wall.

◆ Pull off or unscrew the stem sleeves *(above, right)*.

2. Removing the shower and spout.

◆ Pull the shower escutcheon away from the wall.

◆ With a pipe wrench, unscrew the shower arm *(left)*.

◆ If the tub spout has a setscrew at the base, loosen it and slide the spout off. When it does not have a setscrew, turn the spout counter-clockwise with a pipe wrench.

3. Freeing the tub.
◆ If the tub has a tiled wall, chip away the row of tiles above the tub with a cold chisel and a ball-peen hammer *(left)*, then cut away the wallboard with a wallboard saw. For a molded tub surround, pry off the entire unit.
◆ Demolish the end wall that divides the tub from the rest of the bathroom, cutting off the supply pipes that serve the tub and the shower a few inches above the floor.

4. Disconnecting the drain.
◆ If the bathroom is directly above a basement where you can access the plumbing, work from below the tub. Otherwise, cut a 12-inch-square hole in the floor around the drainpipe.
◆ With channel-joint pliers, loosen the slip nut holding the tub's drain outlet and overflow pipe to the drain tailpiece *(right)*.
◆ Cut the supply pipes to just below floor level.
◆ Take out the screws or nails anchoring the tub flange to the wall studs, then pry the tub from the wall. Recruit helpers to carry or slide it out on a mat or piece of cardboard. Temporarily remove sinks *(pages 27-28)* and toilets *(pages 32-33)* if they are in the way.
◆ Strip the tile and wallboard from the walls surrounding the tub, then put in water-resistant wallboard *(pages 63-65)*.

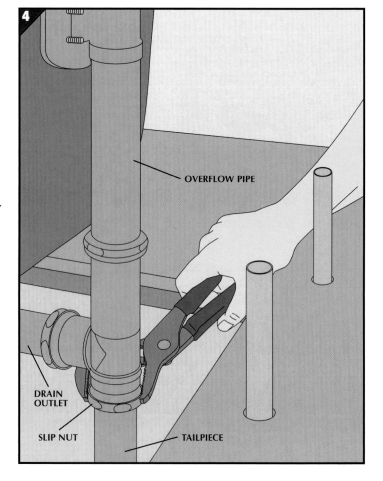

OVERFLOW PIPE

DRAIN OUTLET

SLIP NUT

TAILPIECE

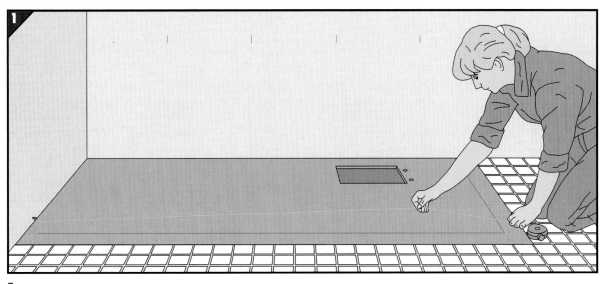

1. Marking the tub position.

◆ Measure the length and width of the new tub, including the lip.

◆ To determine the size of the platform, add the tub dimensions to the desired size of the ledges and subtract 1 inch for the tub lip to overlap the ledges.

◆ Mark the outline roughly on the flooring and cut away the flooring to the nearest tile joint.

◆ Snap chalk lines to outline the precise position of the platform, then snap lines inside the first ones to indicate the thickness of the walls *(above)*—including the width of the studs and $\frac{3}{4}$-inch plywood.

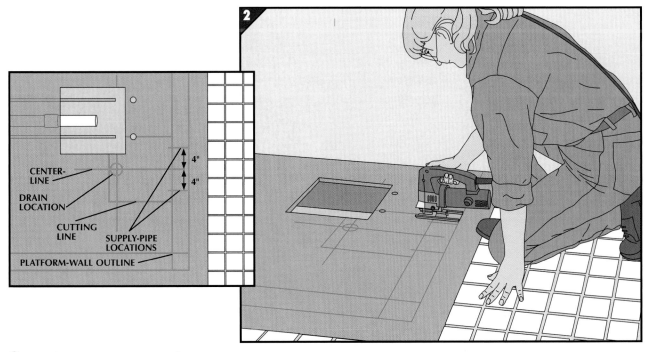

2. Cutting an access opening.

◆ Set the tub in position with its lip at the desired distance from the walls and trace the outline of the drain location on the subfloor, then remove the tub.

◆ As shown in the inset, mark the locations of the pipes and access opening: Draw two intersecting lines 2 feet long through the center of the circle at the drain location. On the platform-wall outline 4 inches to each side of the drain centerline, draw lines to indicate the locations of the supply tubes. Starting at the inside of the platform-wall outline near the supply-tube locations, mark a 12- by 12-inch square access opening centered over the drain centerline.

◆ Drill a $\frac{1}{2}$-inch starter hole on the square outline and cut out the square with a saber saw *(above)*.

3. Moving the drain line.

◆ Evaluate the path the existing drainpipe will need to reach the new tub-drain location. When a floor joist obstructs the new drain line, cut a notch in it for the new pipe.

◆ Cut and test-fit a drainpipe to reach the new drain location, using an elbow to turn the pipe in the right direction *(right)*.

◆ Assemble the drain line with cement *(page 125)*, then support the new drainpipe with a 1-by-2 nailed between joists.

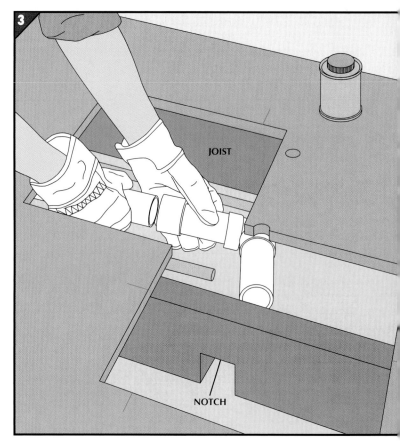

4. Extending the supply pipes.

With couplings, elbows, and additional lengths of supply pipe, run the supply lines to the location marks on the floor and extend them about 6 inches above floor level, supporting them with a 1-by-2 nailed between joists and soldering them *(left)* as explained on page 125.

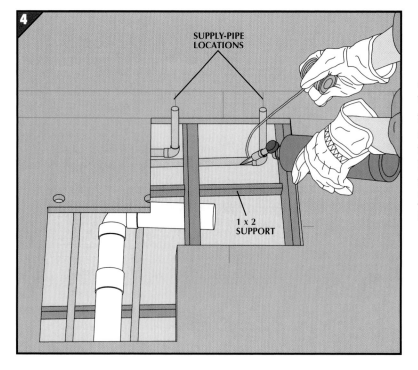

1. Measuring the tub height.

◆ At each corner of the tub, measure up from the floor to the underside of the lip of the tub to find the highest corner *(right)*.

◆ To calculate the height of the platform walls, add together the thickness of the platform's plywood top and the thickness of the tiles to be installed, and subtract this amount from the tub-height measurement.

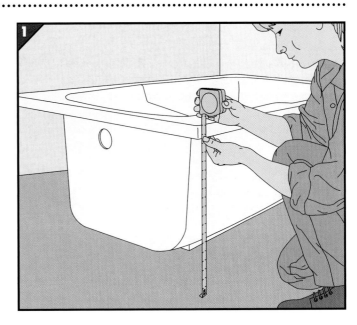

2. Framing the platform.

◆ Build 2-by-4 stud walls *(pages 60-62)* to the length of the open sides of the tub outline and to the height determined in Step 1.

◆ Position the short platform wall over its outline on the floor and add shims to level it. Fasten the wall to the floor with 3-inch nails every 6 to 8 inches. Plumb the wall, then nail it to a stud in the existing wall or secure it with hollow-wall anchors.

◆ Add the second platform wall, level it, and nail it to the floor.

◆ Plumb both platform walls with shims at the corner where they meet *(left)*, fasten the long wall to the existing wall, then nail the two walls to each other.

◆ Cut the shims flush with the walls with a utility knife.

3. Adding the cleats.

◆ With an electronic stud finder, locate and mark the positions of studs along the bathroom walls.

◆ Draw level lines on the walls that correspond to the top of the platform walls.

◆ Cut 2-by-4 cleats to fit between the bathroom walls and the platform walls, then place them at the level lines and attach them at the stud marks with 3-inch nails *(right)*.

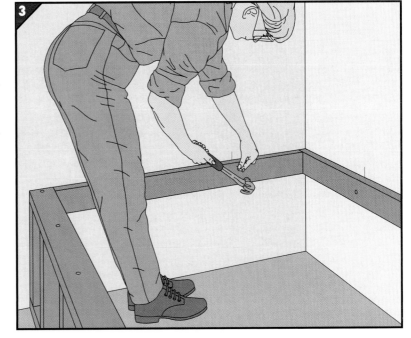

4. Installing the top.

◆ For the platform top, cut a piece of $\frac{3}{4}$-inch exterior-grade plywood large enough to overhang the platform walls by $\frac{3}{4}$ inch.

◆ Flip the tub over onto the plywood, center it, and trace its outline.

◆ Remove the tub and mark a second set of lines 1 inch inside the first to extend the top under the lip of the tub.

◆ Set the plywood in place and fasten it to the platform walls and cleats every 6 inches with $1\frac{1}{4}$-inch nails (right).

◆ Drill a $\frac{1}{2}$-inch starter hole inside the inner outline, then cut along the line with a saber saw.

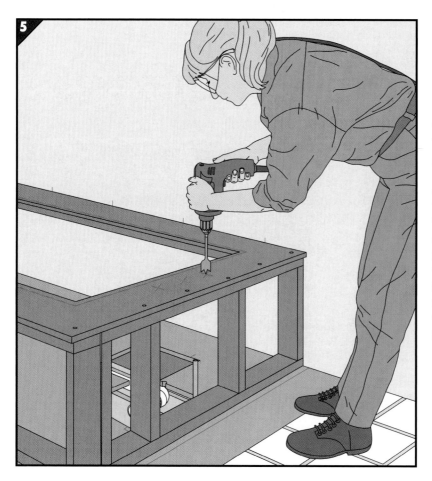

5. Holes for faucets and spout.

◆ Mark the desired location of the faucets and spout on the plywood top, positioning the marks for the faucets roughly above the supply pipes and centering the mark for the spout between them. Make sure the marks are far enough back from the opening to allow room for the tub lip, but are not placed over the platform wall.

◆ Measure the faucet-barrel diameter, fit an electric drill with the appropriate spade bit, and drill the holes (left).

◆ Drill the hole for the spout in the same way.

6. Tiling the platform.

◆ If you have cut the flooring back more than 1 inch from the platform walls, patch it.

◆ Cut a piece of $\frac{3}{4}$-inch exterior plywood for the long platform wall; fit it under the overhanging top piece and fasten it to the studs with $1\frac{1}{4}$-inch nails every 6 inches.

◆ Using the straight edge of a notched trowel, spread a thin layer of latex-modified thinset mortar recommended for plywood on the surfaces and let it set for about two hours. Apply a second coat, allowing the teeth of the trowel to penetrate to the plywood.

◆ Starting at one corner, lay tiles on the top of the platform, using the spacers or built-in lugs to position them. If needed, cut tiles with a tile cutter to fit along the walls and tub opening. At the spout and faucet locations, cut tiles in half and make semicircles with nippers *(inset)*.

◆ Starting at a top corner, tile the side of the platform *(left)* without overlapping the top tiles.

◆ For the removable end panel, fit plywood and tile it in the same way as the side wall but without adhesive at the top edge. At the corner, bring the tiles to the long side but do not overlap them. Once the adhesive sets, remove the panel.

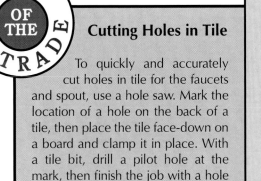

TRICKS OF THE TRADE

Cutting Holes in Tile

To quickly and accurately cut holes in tile for the faucets and spout, use a hole saw. Mark the location of a hole on the back of a tile, then place the tile face-down on a board and clamp it in place. With a tile bit, drill a pilot hole at the mark, then finish the job with a hole saw *(right)*.

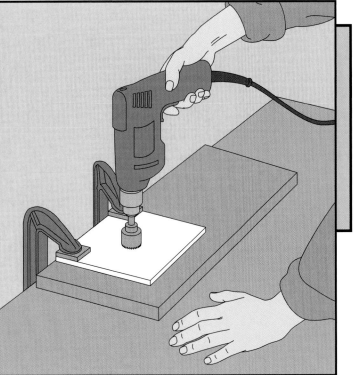

7. Grouting the tiles.

◆ Spread a cup or two of latex-modified tile grout onto the tiles and drag it diagonally across the joints with a rubber grout float, pressing it into the joints *(left)*.

◆ Wait 15 minutes, then wipe off excess with a damp sponge.

◆ Let the grout set for the time specified by the manufacturer, then wipe any haze off the tiles with a soft cloth.

◆ Fill the perimeter joints of the platform with silicone caulk.

◆ Once the grout has fully cured, brush on a grout sealer.

CONNECTING THE PLUMBING

1. Putting in the tub.

◆ Prepare a batch of pre-mixed mortar and spread it 2 to 4 inches thick on the subfloor inside the platform.

◆ With a helper, place the tub in the opening in the platform *(right)*. Get into the tub to seat it firmly, then check it for level.

◆ Run a bead of caulk around the lip of the tub where it meets the tile.

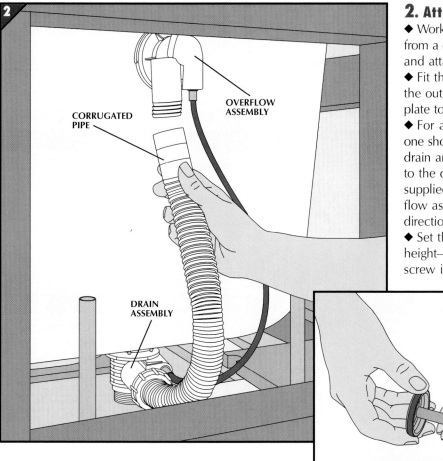

2. Attaching the overflow.

◆ Working with a helper, fit the drain assembly from a drain and overflow kit under the tub drain and attach the drain's crosspiece inside the tub.

◆ Fit the overflow assembly into its hole from the outside of the tub and fasten the overflow plate to it from inside the tub.

◆ For a corrugated overflow pipe such as the one shown here, cut the pipe to fit between the drain and overflow assemblies. Attach one end to the drain assembly with the compression nut supplied and push the other end onto the overflow assembly *(left)*. Follow the manufacturer's directions for other types of overflow pipe.

◆ Set the stopper into the strainer and adjust its height—on this model, by raising or lowering the screw in the bottom of the stopper's stem *(inset)*.

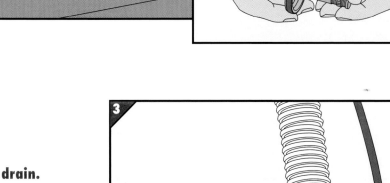

3. Hooking up the drain.

◆ Fasten the tailpiece provided with the drain kit to the bottom of the drain assembly with the slip nut supplied.

◆ Cement *(page 125)* a trap adapter to the lower end of a P-trap.

◆ Test-fit the trap and, if necessary, cut the tailpiece or new horizontal section of drainpipe to the appropriate length.

◆ Reinstall the trap, cementing the horizontal section to the new drainpipe and tightening the slip nut of the trap adapter over the tailpiece *(right)*.

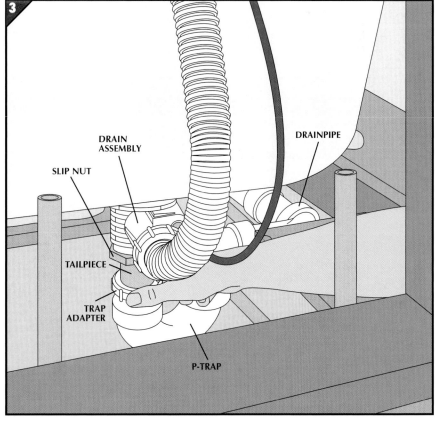

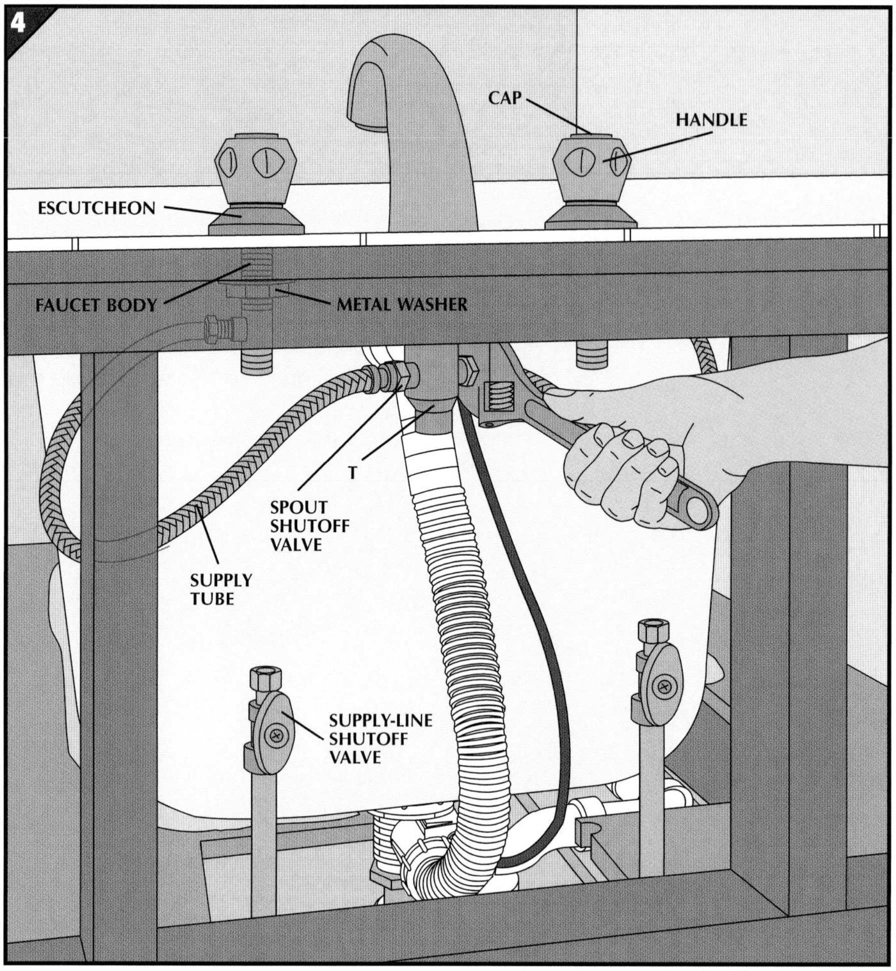

4. Adding faucets and spout.
◆ Slip a nut and metal washer over one faucet body and insert it from below into the hole in the platform. Add a rubber washer, metal washer, and nut from the top, then tighten the nuts. Position the escutcheon and handle on the faucet, tighten the screw in the handle, and snap on the cap. Install the other valve body and handle in the same way.
◆ Pass the stem of the spout through its hole in the platform from above, add a metal washer and nut, and tighten the nut, then screw on the T.
◆ Solder *(page 125)* a pair of shutoff valves to the ends of the supply pipes.
◆ Run flexible supply tubes between the faucets and spout shutoff valves, tightening the nuts a quarter-turn with an open-end wrench *(left)*.
◆ Attach flexible supply tubes to the faucets and the supply-line shutoff valves *(page 35, Step 4)*.

Labels in figure:
CAP
HANDLE
ESCUTCHEON
FAUCET BODY
METAL WASHER
T
SPOUT SHUTOFF VALVE
SUPPLY TUBE
SUPPLY-LINE SHUTOFF VALVE

5. Attaching the access panel.
◆ Position the panel over the end of the platform.
◆ Drill holes through grout joints for six $1\frac{1}{2}$-inch No. 8 screws, locating the holes so they penetrate the top and bottom plates or the studs of the platform wall.
◆ Slip a decorative cup washer *(photograph)* over each screw and fasten the panel to the platform through the holes *(right)*.

WIRING A WHIRLPOOL

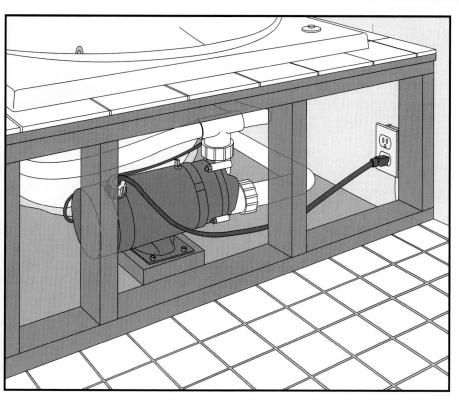

A platform installation.

This whirlpool is designed to be installed in a raised platform like the one shown on pages 87 to 94. The plumbing connections are at one end of the whirlpool and are similar to those of a regular tub. The motor is at the other end of the tub. Access panels are required for both the plumbing and motor. Whirlpools like the model shown here simply plug into an outlet on a dedicated circuit protected at the service panel by a ground-fault circuit interrupter (GFCI) breaker.

Wiring the outlet.

◆ Drill a hole into the wallboard inside the tub platform and fish electrical cable to it from the service-panel location *(page 121)*.
◆ Pull the cable through a knockout in an electrical box and clamp it securely, attach the box to a stud inside the platform at least 4 inches from the floor *(right)*, and prepare the wires *(pages 121-122)*.
◆ Connect a standard duplex receptacle by attaching the cable's black wire to the brass terminal screw on the receptacle and the white wire to the silver terminal. For a metal box, attach a green jumper to the ground screw on the receptacle and another to the grounding screw on the box; join the two jumpers to the cable's copper ground wire with a wire cap *(inset)*. For a plastic box, omit the jumper to the box.
◆ Have an electrician install a GFCI breaker at the service panel and hook up the new circuit.

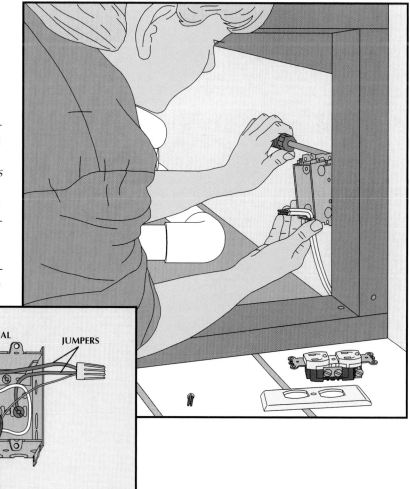

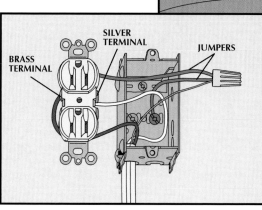

BRASS TERMINAL

SILVER TERMINAL

JUMPERS

The Ultimate Luxury: A Steam Bath

Except for its insulating dome and door that seal in heat, a steam-bath stall is similar to a standard shower unit, and functions as both shower and steam bath. The model on these pages is designed for a corner installation; steam baths that fit three-sided alcoves are also available.

Replacing a Shower: If the existing shower stall is a different size than the steam-bath unit, you may need to relocate the pipes for the drain and water supply. To shift the drainpipe, open up the bathroom floor *(page 86, Step 4)*

or access the plumbing from the ceiling of the room below it. The tools and materials you'll need for connecting pipe are listed on page 123.

When the existing shower has a molded surround, simply remove it first *(page 97)*. If the walls of the shower are tiled, strip off the tile and wallboard and place the new stall against the wall studs.

Plumbing the Generator: Steam for the unit is produced in a generator, which can be housed in the basement under the bathroom, in an attic, in a

closet, or at any location near your home's water-supply pipes. When the distance from the generator to the steam head is more than 10 feet, place steam-rated insulation around the pipes to retain the heat. The pipes between the generator and steam head can be run horizontally, up, or down; but do not route them down first, then up.

> ⚠️ **CAUTION** *Before cutting into walls, check for the presence of asbestos and lead (page 43).*

 TOOLS

Hacksaw	Channel-joint pliers	Electric drill
Wallboard saw	Adjustable wrenches	Carpenter's level
Circular saw	Screwdrivers	Fish tape
Saber saw	Hammer	Cable ripper
Utility knife	Rubber mallet	Electrician's multipurpose tool
Pry bar	Putty knife	Caulking gun

 **MATERIALS**

Steam-bath shower unit	Electrical box and 20-amp outlet	Two-part shower drain
2 x 2s, 2 x 4s	Wire caps	Plumber's putty
Plywood ($\frac{1}{2}$")	Supply pipe and fittings	Common nails ($3\frac{1}{2}$")
Shims	Shutoff valve	Wood screws (3" No. 8)
Electrical cable	Drainpipe and fittings	Wallboard screws ($1\frac{1}{4}$")
		Silicone caulk

 **SAFETY TIPS**

Wear goggles when cutting, drilling, or hammering. Add gloves when using a propane torch. When soldering, put a flameproof pad behind the work and keep a fire extinguisher nearby.

A steam-bath stall.
The two-section unit of molded fiberglass and acrylic at left has two glass side panels and a glass door. An acrylic dome seals the top of the stall. A shower head and faucet, centered in a wall panel, are installed at the desired heights, and the steam head is located near the floor of the stall, far enough away from the seat to prevent scalding. The control pad is situated at a convenient height.

DOME

SHOWER HEAD

CONTROL PAD

SHOWER FAUCET

FIXED PANEL

STEAM HEAD

SEAT

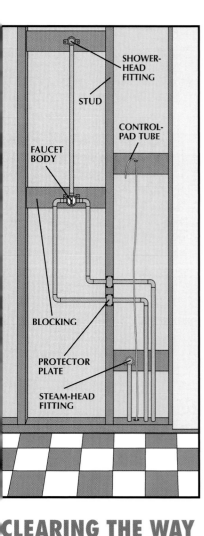

Plumbing the steam bath.

The bathroom wall at the site for the steam bath is opened to accommodate the stall and its plumbing *(left)*. The shower head, faucet body, steam head, and pneumatic tube to the control pad are secured to 2-by-4 blocking nailed on-edge between studs. When studs are notched to fit pipes, metal plates protect the pipes and reinforce the studs. If necessary, a stud is added at each edge of the opening as a fastening surface for the stall.

Installing the generator.

In the illustration at right, the steam generator is placed on a platform suspended from ceiling joists in the basement. A supply pipe with a shutoff valve connects the generator to the cold-water line of the house; a second pipe routes water from the generator to the steam head in the stall. Cable for a new 20-amp 120-volt circuit runs from the service panel to an outlet that the generator is plugged into. A pneumatic tube links the generator to the control pad in the stall.

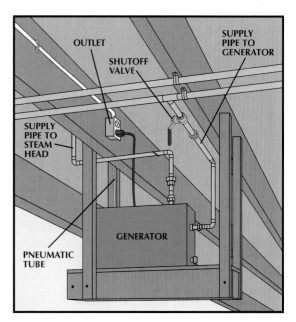

CLEARING THE WAY

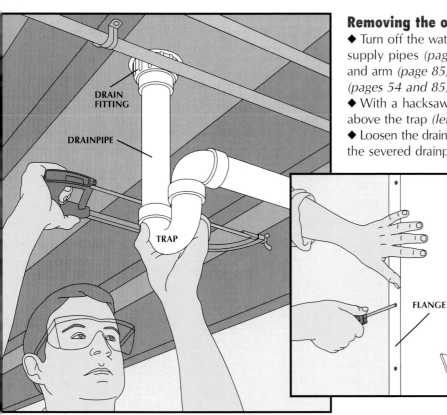

Removing the old shower unit.

◆ Turn off the water supply to the bathroom and drain the supply pipes *(page 124)*, then remove the shower head and arm *(page 85)* and the faucet handles and escutcheons *(pages 54 and 85)*.
◆ With a hacksaw, cut through the shower's drainpipe just above the trap *(left)*.
◆ Loosen the drain fitting with channel-joint pliers and remove the severed drainpipe.
◆ Cut the horizontal length of drainpipe close to the trap and remove the trap.
◆ Pull the drain out of the stall.
◆ Remove any trim at the stall edges, then unscrew the flanges *(inset)*.
◆ Pry the stall away from the walls and take it out of the bathroom.

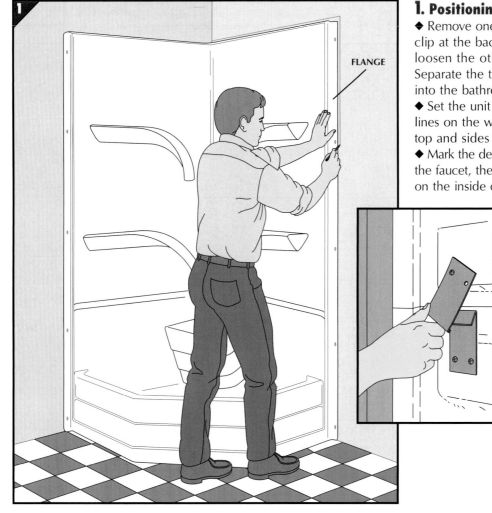

FLANGE

1. Positioning the unit.

◆ Remove one screw from the top half of each clip at the back of the steam-bath wall panels, loosen the other, and swivel the clip *(inset)*. Separate the two stall sections and move them into the bathroom, then reassemble them.

◆ Set the unit into place and level it, then draw lines on the walls along the outer flanges at the top and sides *(left)*.

◆ Mark the desired locations of the shower head, the faucet, the steam head, and the control pad on the inside of the stall.

2. Moving supply pipes.

◆ Pull out the stall and cut away the wallboard between the marks on the walls. If there are no studs at the edges of the opening, toenail new studs there as fastening surfaces for the stall flanges and secure the cut edges of the wallboard to them with $1\frac{1}{4}$-inch wallboard screws.

◆ Transfer the locations of the shower head, faucet, steam head, and control pad from the shower stall to the wallboard behind the studs, then nail blocking made of 2-by-4s set on-edge between the backs of the studs at the marks.

◆ Cut the existing supply pipes, then solder *(pages 124-125)* new lengths of pipe using elbows and couplings to extend them to the blockings for the plumbing fittings *(right)*.

◆ Move the existing faucet body and shower fitting to the new positions or install new ones.

◆ Secure the ends of the pipes to the blocking with pipe clamps.

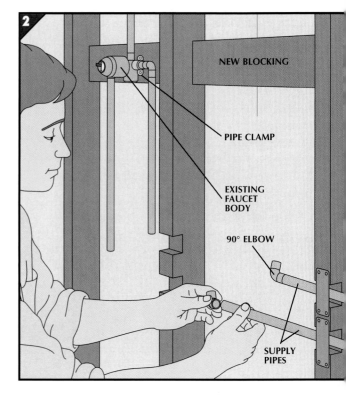

NEW BLOCKING

PIPE CLAMP

EXISTING FAUCET BODY

90° ELBOW

SUPPLY PIPES

SETTING UP THE GENERATOR

1. Assembling a platform.

◆ Choose a convenient location near the supply pipes for the generator—here, in an unfinished basement.

◆ Build a platform for the generator out of 2-by-4s and $\frac{1}{2}$-inch plywood, assembling the pieces with 3-inch No. 8 wood screws.

◆ Working with a helper, hang the platform level from the ceiling joists with 2-by-2s, screwing them to the frame and the joists (left).

◆ Place the generator on the platform.

2. Tapping into the supply pipe.

◆ Cut the cold-water supply pipe near the water inlet on the generator, then attach a T-fitting, a short length of supply pipe, a shutoff valve, and another short length of pipe using the cutting and fitting techniques on pages 123 to 125.

◆ Open the main water-supply valve about a quarter of the way, then open the shutoff valve and allow water to flow into a bucket for few minutes to flush the line. Turn off the water.

◆ Connect a threaded adapter to the generator's water inlet and, using elbows where required, run pipe to meet the open pipe at the shutoff valve.

◆ Link the two sections of pipe with a union (page 123), tightening it with two adjustable wrenches (right).

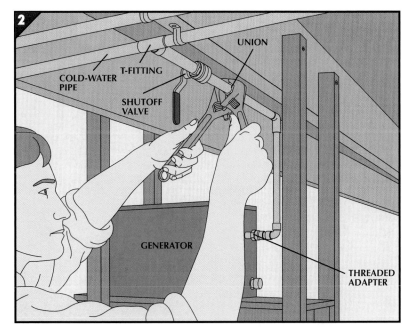

PROTECTING THE GENERATOR WITH A WATER FILTER

Sediment and deposits in water can damage a steam generator. The water in most towns is relatively free of these contaminants, but if you get your water from a well you may need to add a filter. Consult the generator manufacturer to find out what type you need. An in-line water filter (photograph) that removes silt can be installed on the generator's supply pipe just past the shutoff valve. If the water is extremely hard, you may need a phosphate filter as well. Brass compression fittings connect the filter to the line, and it is placed in the water-flow direction indicated by the arrow on its housing. Replace the filter cartridge periodically, in accordance with the manufacturer's requirements.

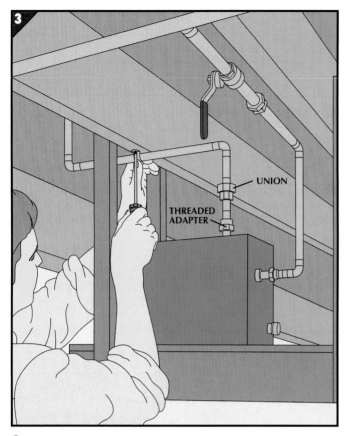

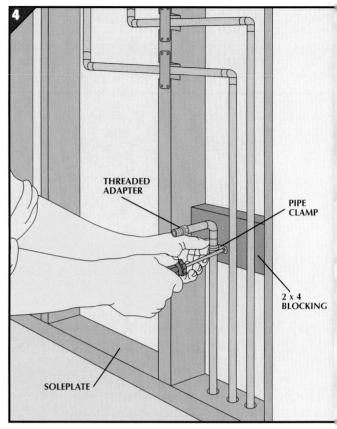

3. Running pipe to the bathroom.
◆ Connect a threaded adapter to the generator's water outlet, then a short length of pipe and a union.
◆ Run pipe up to the level of the bottom of the joists and then horizontally to the desired location.
◆ Wherever the pipe crosses a ceiling joist, attach it with a pipe clamp *(above)*. If the pipe runs parallel to the joists, install blocking between the joists and clamp the pipe to the blocking.

4. Installing the steam-head fitting.
◆ Drill a hole through the soleplate and continue the run of pipe from the generator to the blocking for the steam head *(page 98, Step 2)*.
◆ Install a 90-degree elbow and a male-threaded adapter at the end of the pipe. With a pipe clamp, secure the pipe to the blocking *(above)*.

5. Wiring the generator.
◆ Screw an electrical box to a ceiling joist or wall stud near the generator, within reach of its power cord, and run cable to it from the main service panel *(page 121)*, but do not hook up the new circuit.
◆ Clamp the cable to the box and prepare the wires *(pages 121-122)*, then install a 20-amp receptacle *(right)*, wiring it in the same way as an ordinary receptacle *(page 95)*. Have an electrician hook up the new circuit to a ground-fault circuit interrupter (GFCI) breaker at the service panel.
◆ Run the pneumatic hose from the generator to the steam-bath location and secure it to the blocking. Cut the hose to length with a utility knife, leaving it long enough to pass through the wall of the shower stall.

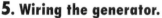

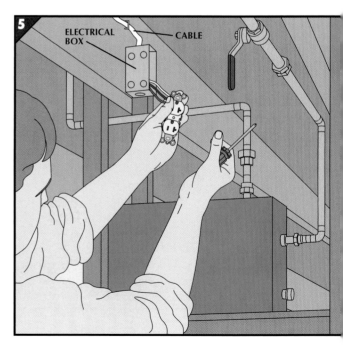

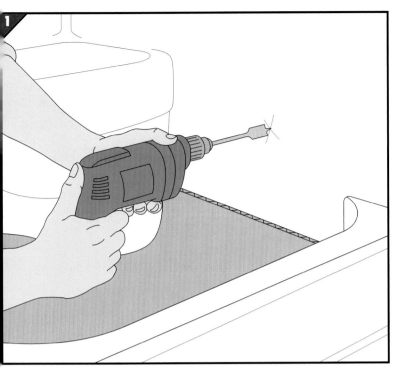

1. Drilling the fixture holes.
◆ Protect the floor of the shower stall with cardboard.
◆ At the locations marked on the stall for the faucet, steam head, and control pad, drill holes of the size recommended by the manufacturer *(left)*.
◆ For the shower arm, drill a 1-inch-diameter hole.

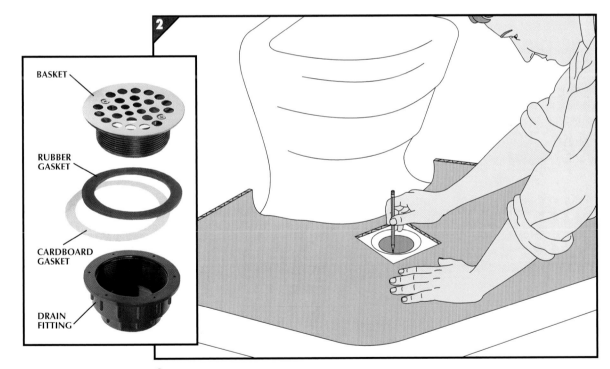

BASKET

RUBBER GASKET

CARDBOARD GASKET

DRAIN FITTING

2. Installing the drain.
◆ Set the stall in position and trace the drain opening onto the subfloor *(above)*, then lay the stall on its side, taking it apart if necessary *(page 98, Step 1)*.
◆ Disassemble a two-part shower drain *(photograph)*, then apply plumber's putty to the bottom of the basket and press it into the drain hole from inside the stall.
◆ From the underside of the stall, slip the rubber gasket followed by the cardboard gasket onto the basket, then thread on the drain fitting and tighten it with a pipe wrench.
◆ Drill a starter hole through the center of the drain location marked on the subfloor, then cut out the circle with a saber saw.

3. Positioning the unit.

◆ Move the stall into place, aligning plumbing fittings and holes, and pass the pneumatic tube for the control pad through its hole. Adjust the unit so the stall flanges rest against the studs and fit snugly at the edges of the wallboard.

◆ With a carpenter's level, check the unit for plumb and level. Hammer in shims on both sides of the front of the base to level the unit *(right)*.

◆ With a utility knife, trim the shims flush with the base of the stall.

◆ Fasten the unit by driving $1\frac{1}{4}$-inch wallboard screws through the holes in the flanges into the studs.

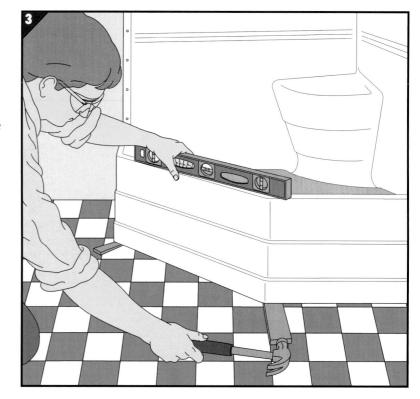

TRICKS OF THE TRADE

Stabilizing the Unit

The thin, flexible walls of some shower stalls can seem unsubstantial. To add sturdiness, fill the space between the stall and the studs with foam-rubber gaskets—available in most hardware centers. Choose gaskets slightly thicker than the space between the flanges and the concave back of the stall—usually $1\frac{1}{2}$ to 2 inches. Before you install the unit, attach the gaskets to the studs wherever they will come into contact with the shower walls *(below)*. Most gaskets have adhesive strips, but for added stability, also nail them every 12 to 16 inches to the studs. Once the stall is in place, it will compress the gaskets.

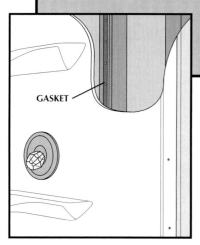

GASKET

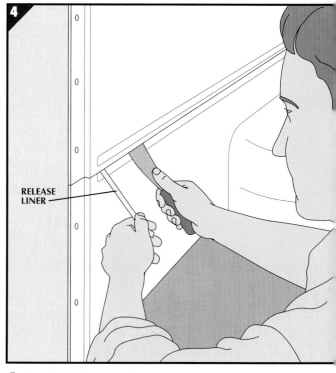

RELEASE LINER

4. Sealing the sections.

◆ On one side of the unit, grasp the release liner covering the adhesive strip between the stall sections and peel it back about 4 inches.

◆ Pry apart the joint with a small putty knife and strip the release liner *(above)*, working your way along the entire length of the joint. Remove the release liner on the other wall of the unit in the same way.

◆ Press the joint together to adhere the two sections.

5. Hooking up the fixtures.

◆ Reverse the procedures described on pages 54 and 85 to install the faucets and shower head.

◆ Slip the escutcheon over the threaded adapter for the steam head, then thread on the steam head *(right)*.

◆ Working from the basement, extend the cut drain lines to the new location *(page 88)*.

◆ Cement a straight length of pipe to the shower's drain fitting. Then, test-fit and install a trap as shown on page 93, Step 3, but cementing both ends.

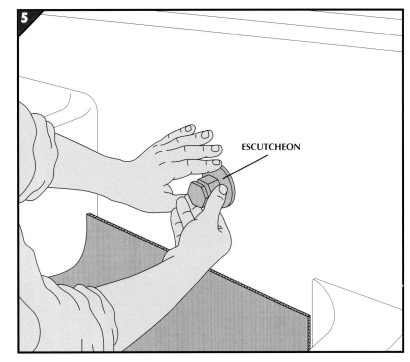

6. Installing the control pad.

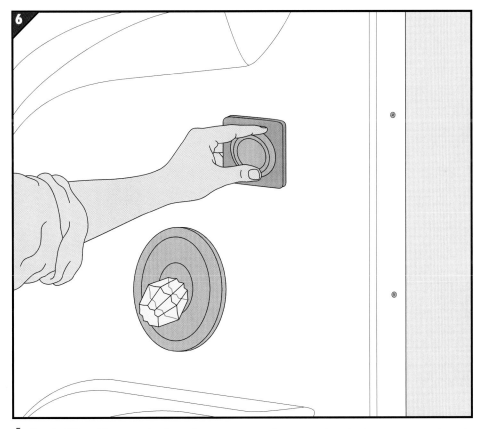

◆ Attach the pneumatic hose to the back of the control pad.

◆ Plug the generator into its receptacle.

◆ Restore the water supply and test the generator by pressing the steam button on the control pad. If steam is produced within a few minutes, turn off the steam and apply silicone adhesive to the back of the control pad, then press it against the wall of the stall *(above)*. Wait 24 hours before using the unit.

HANGING THE GLASS PANELS AND DOOR

1. Attaching the channels.

◆ Place one of the bottom channels along the base on one side of the unit flush against the wall. With the setup jig provided, space the channel uniformly from the edge *(inset)*, then mark the positions of the predrilled holes.

◆ Remove the channel and drill holes of the size specified at the marks. Reposition the channel and drive the screws.

◆ Fit a wall channel into the bottom channel and position its top with the jig, then screw it in place *(right)*. Install the other channels in the same way.

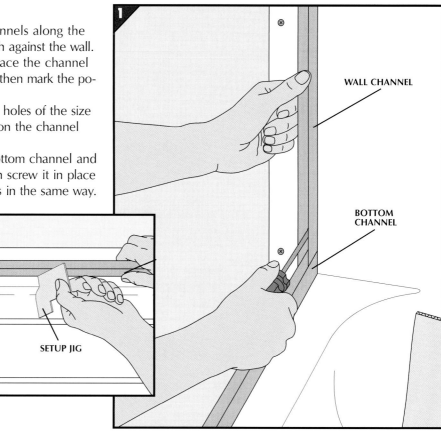

WALL CHANNEL

BOTTOM CHANNEL

SETUP JIG

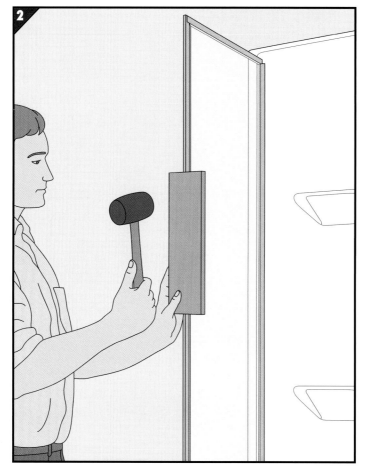

2. Installing the glass panels.

◆ Apply soapy water to the panel gaskets and slide them onto the edges of the fixed panels.

◆ Place one end of a fixed panel into the corner where the wall and bottom channels meet. Tilt it into position, sliding the gaskets into the channels.

◆ Place a wood block on the exposed edge of the panel and tap it with a rubber mallet to seat it *(left)*. Tap down on the top of the panel.

◆ Install the second fixed panel in the same way.

3. Putting in the top rail.

◆ Assemble the top rail by fastening the three sections together with the brackets and screws provided *(inset)*.

◆ Place the assembled rail on top of the fixed panels and gently tap it into place *(right)*.

◆ Being careful not to drill into the glass, drill holes of the specified size through the holes in the top rail into the top of the wall channels.

◆ Secure the top rail with screws.

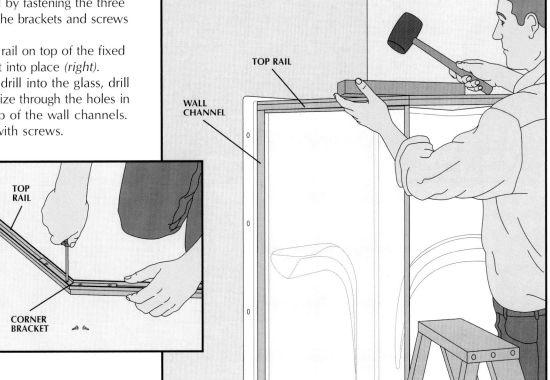

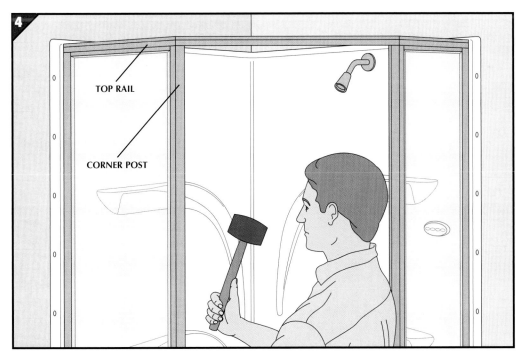

4. Adding the corner posts.

◆ Place a corner post on the open end of a fixed panel, starting at the bottom and tilting it into place. Tap the post with a rubber mallet along its length.

◆ Drill holes of the specified size through the holes at the top and bottom of the corner post into the top rail and bottom channel, then drive the screws provided.

◆ Install the second post *(above)*.

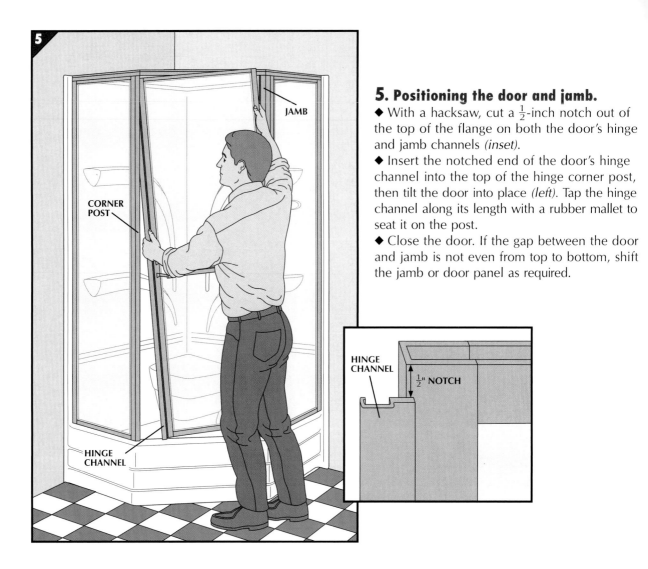

5. Positioning the door and jamb.

◆ With a hacksaw, cut a $\frac{1}{2}$-inch notch out of the top of the flange on both the door's hinge and jamb channels *(inset)*.

◆ Insert the notched end of the door's hinge channel into the top of the hinge corner post, then tilt the door into place *(left)*. Tap the hinge channel along its length with a rubber mallet to seat it on the post.

◆ Close the door. If the gap between the door and jamb is not even from top to bottom, shift the jamb or door panel as required.

6. Mounting the header bar.

◆ Slide the header bar into the top rail above the door *(right)*.

◆ Close the door and adjust the header so there is an even $\frac{1}{16}$-inch gap between the door and header.

◆ Drill holes of the specified size through the holes on the inside of the top rail into the header and drive the screws.

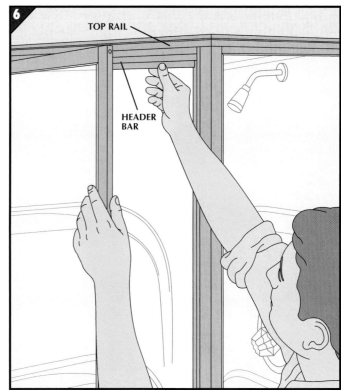

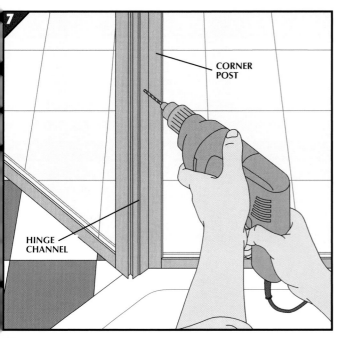

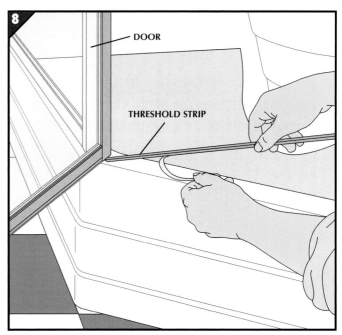

7. Securing the door.
◆ Drill holes of the specified size through the holes on the inside of the corner post into the hinge channel *(above)* and drive the screws.
◆ Fasten the jamb channel in the same way.
◆ Install the towel rack on the outside of the door and the handle on the inside, driving the screws into the predrilled holes on the door frame.

8. Laying the threshold strip.
◆ Measure the space between the corner posts and, with a hacksaw, trim the threshold strip to fit.
◆ Peel off the adhesive backing-paper and fix the strip into place, its angled slope toward the inside of the unit *(above)*.

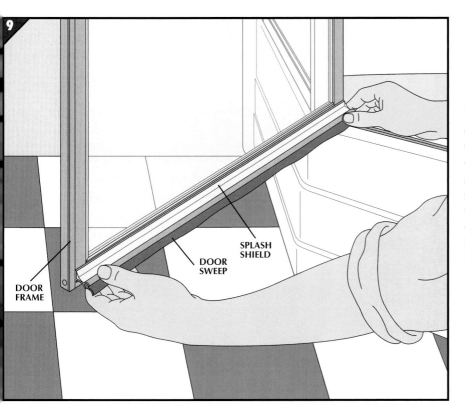

9. Installing the splash shield.
◆ Slide the door sweep into place on the splash shield.
◆ Peel off the adhesive backing-paper and stick the splash shield onto the in-side of the door at the bottom of the frame *(left)*.
◆ Fit the plastic water dam into the high end of the splash shield, adhering it with a dab of silicone caulk.

FINISHING THE STALL

1. Attaching J-molding.
◆ With a carpenter's level, mark a level line along the top of the stall unit in line with the top of the top rail.
◆ Peel the adhesive backing-paper off the J molding and align the top of the molding with the marked line, then press it in place.
◆ Apply a bead of silicone caulk along the inside of the channel on the top rail and the J-molding (right).

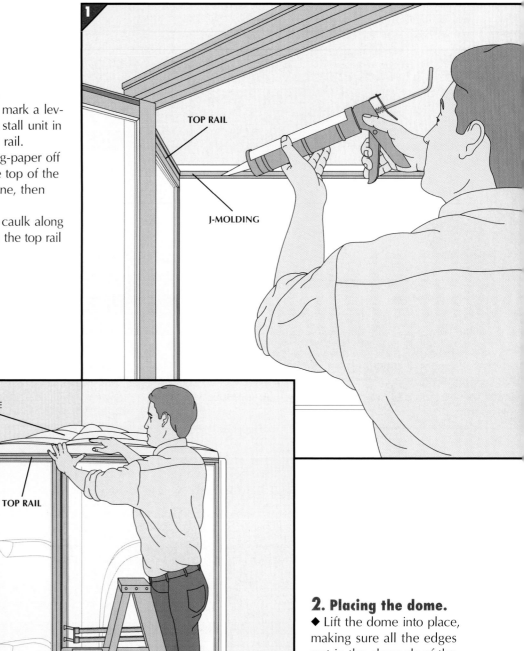

2. Placing the dome.
◆ Lift the dome into place, making sure all the edges rest in the channels of the J-molding and top rail.
◆ From above, press the edges of the dome down into the caulk (left).

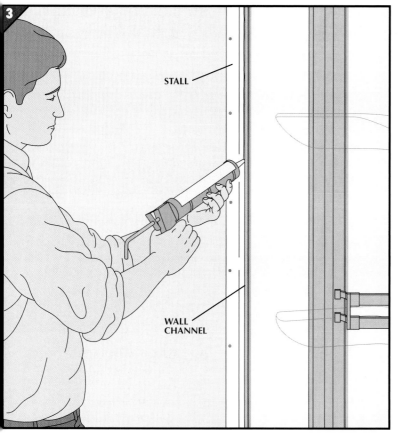

STALL

WALL
CHANNEL

3. Applying caulk.

◆ Run a bead of silicone caulk at the joint where the channels meet the shower stall *(left)*.

◆ Seal the gap between the floor and the unit with a bead of silicone caulk, hiding the edges of the shims.

◆ Cut lengths of wood molding to cover the flanges of the stall and fasten it to the wallboard with $1\frac{1}{2}$-inch finishing nails driven every foot.

A SAUNA FROM A KIT

A dry sauna—essentially an insulated, wood-lined room—can be easily assembled from one of the variety of kits available. The wood in the kit is kiln-dried and aromatic—typically redwood or western red cedar. The model at right includes preassembled wall panels, a pre-hung door, insulation, siding, a 2-by-4 base, and a 2-by-2 frame. The unit comes with pre-fabricated benches and igneous stones that re-tain heat and moisture. A dedicated 220-amp circuit is required for the heater unit, which in-cludes a built-in or wall-mounted thermostat with a 60-minute timer.

Even on a winter morning, your bathroom floor can be toasty warm with a radiant-heat system like the one on these pages. Its network of cables keeps the floor at a constant and uniform temperature.

Getting Ready: Available at home-supply centers, radiant-heat systems come in kits that include heating cables and a thermostat and the hardware for installing them. Before you order one, check local codes for any restrictions on its installation. Then, find the square footage of the floor so you can buy a kit with the correct number and length of heating cables. The next step is to clear the way for installation of the system. Take out the sink *(pages 27-28)* and toilet *(pages 32-33)*, then remove the finish floor.

Wiring and Flooring: A radiant-heat system needs a dedicated circuit routed back to the service panel. Have an electrician install a ground-fault circuit interrupter (GFCI) breaker at the service panel and do the hookup there. The tools and materials you'll need for the rest of the wiring are are listed on pages 119 to 122.

The new finish floor must be made of a material that will not discolor from heat, split, or obstruct the distribution of warmth. Ceramic tile is a good choice, and may be recommended by the manufacturer of the system.

⚠ **CAUTION** *Before cutting into flooring or walls, test for lead and asbestos (page 43), and take the necessary safeguards.*

 TOOLS

Stud finder
Utility knife
Wallboard saw
Screwdriver
Hammer
Electric drill

Wood chisel
Straightedge
Notched trowel
Fish tape
Cable ripper
Electrician's
   multipurpose tool
Multitester

 **MATERIALS**

Radiant-heat
  flooring kit
Electrical cable

Metal guard plate
Electrical tape
Premixed mortar
Wallboard ($\frac{1}{2}$")
Wallboard
  screws ($1\frac{1}{2}$")

 **SAFETY TIPS**

Wear goggles when cutting, drilling, or hammering. Protect your hands from contact with wet mortar by putting on work gloves.

A radiant-heat installation.

The system at right consists of a network of heating cables fastened to the subfloor with plastic clips. The cables are laid in a zigzag pattern in the walked-on area of the room; an empty border is left between the cables and plumbing fixtures. A temperature sensor set in the floor is wired to a thermostat in the wall. Electrical cable for a new 20-amp 120-volt circuit connects the thermostat to a GFCI circuit breaker at the service panel. Once the installation is complete, the heating cables are buried in a mortar bed and covered with a suitable finish-floor material.

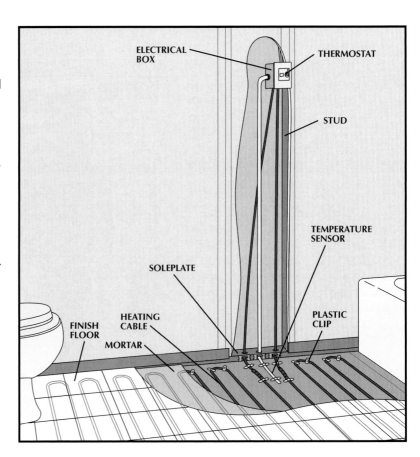

1. Installing the electrical box.

◆ Find the nearest wall studs on each side of the planned site for the thermostat, then cut away a section of wallboard between the stud centers from the floor to a height of 4 to 5 feet.

◆ With a screwdriver, open a knockout on the top of the electrical box provided in the kit, two on the bottom of the box, and one on the side.

◆ Place the electrical box against one of the studs about 4 feet off the floor, then strike the flange with a hammer to drive the teeth into the stud *(left)*.

◆ Run electrical cable of the type recommended by the kit manufacturer to the box *(page 121)* from the service panel location.

◆ At the box, feed the cable into the top knockout, clamp it, and prepare the wires *(pages 121-122)*.

2. Boring holes in the soleplate.

◆ With a $\frac{3}{4}$-inch spade bit, drill three holes into the side of the soleplate about halfway through, centering one between the studs and positioning the other two 4 inches to each side of the first.

◆ Drill a hole into the top of the soleplate to meet each side hole; at the center location, drill two holes next to each other *(right)*.

◆ With a wood chisel, clear out the waste between the two adjacent center holes to create one large hole.

◆ Place a notched metal guard plate *(photograph)* over each hole drilled into the side of the soleplate and strike the plate with a hammer to drive the teeth into the wood.

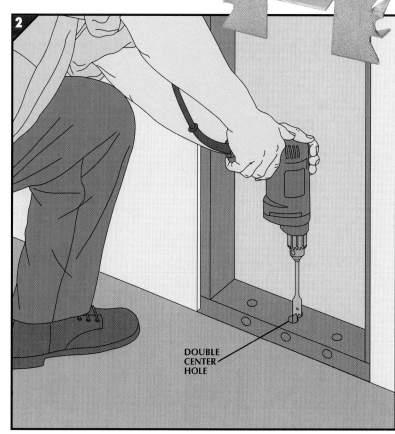

DOUBLE
CENTER
HOLE

LAYING THE CABLE

1. Marking the border.
◆ Consult the manufacturer's instructions to determine the correct border size for the square footage of the flooring area to be covered.
◆ With a straightedge, mark a border at the appropriate distance from each fixture onto the subfloor *(right)*.

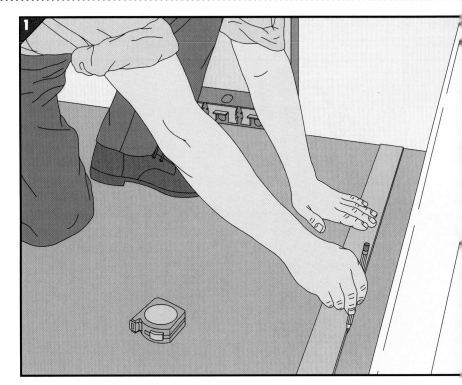

SPLICE

2. Feeding cable into the box.
◆ Unwind enough heating cable from the spool to expose the splice between the lead and heating cable.
◆ Feed the cable through one of the outer holes in the soleplate *(left)* and up through one of the bottom knockouts on the electrical box.

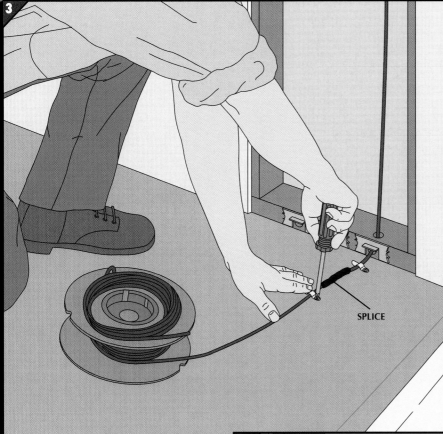

3. Securing the cable.

◆ Adjust the heating cable on the floor until the splice is within 12 inches of the guard plate, then clamp the cable to the electrical box.

◆ Position a plastic clip over the cable on each side of the splice. Fasten one end of each clip to the subfloor with the screws provided *(left)*.

4. Marking clip locations.

◆ Set the spacing template against the wall, aligning one of the heating-cable pictures on the template with the actual cable. Make a mark on the subfloor at each hole in the template *(right)*.

◆ Moving the template end-to-end, mark the clip locations along the entire length of the wall between the border lines in the same manner.

◆ Mark the clip locations along the other side of the room by positioning the template against the opposite wall or border line.

◆ Fasten a clip to the subfloor at each marked location.

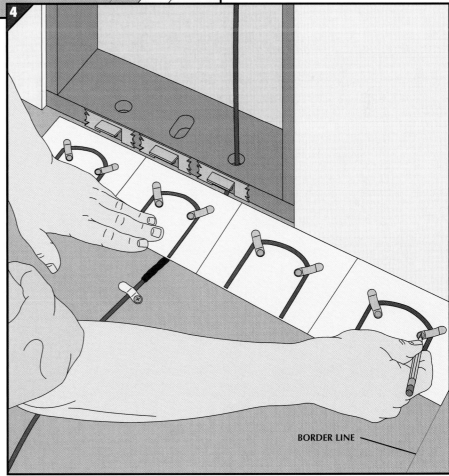

5. Laying the cable.

Weave the heating cable back and forth across the subfloor under the clips *(right)*, following the pattern marked on the template. When you reach the tag on the cable indicating the middle of the run, plan your route back to the wall opening using the cable that remains. Make sure that the cable does not touch or cross itself.

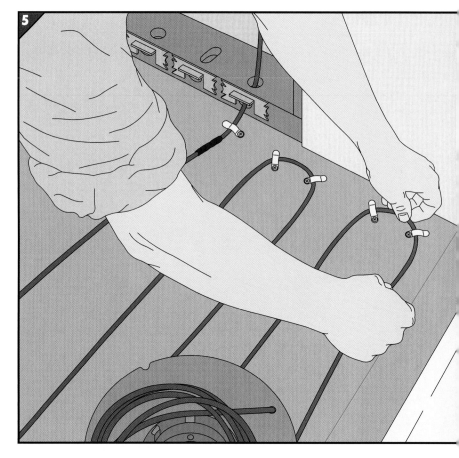

6. Routing cable back to the box.

◆ When you have completed the layout and returned to the wall opening, push the end of the cable through the second outer hole in the soleplate *(left)* and feed it up to the electrical box.

◆ Pass the cable through the second knockout in the bottom of the box, adjust it until the splice is within 12 inches of the soleplate, and clamp it to the box.

◆ Secure the cable to the subfloor with a clip on each side of the splice *(page 113, Step 3)*.

Where a large floor requires two runs of heating cable, feed the first cable out and back through the same hole in the soleplate, and the second cable out and back through the other *(inset)*.

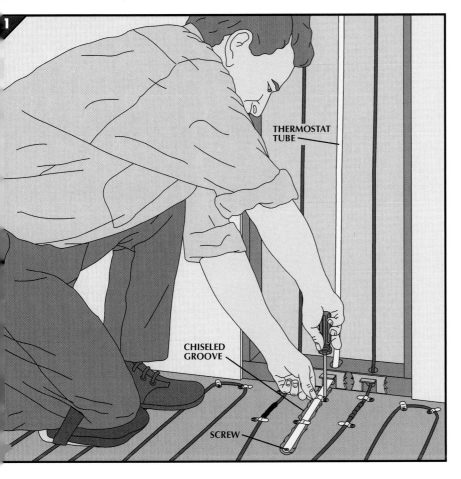

1. Placing the thermostat tube.

◆ Starting at the center hole in the soleplate, chisel a groove in the sub-floor $\frac{1}{2}$ inch wide, $\frac{1}{4}$ inch deep, and 6 inches long.

◆ Screw the kit's plastic bushing into a knockout on the side of the electrical box, then feed the sealed end of the thermostat tube through the bushing and out of the box.

◆ Pass the sealed end of the thermostat tube through the soleplate's center hole and into the chiseled groove.

◆ Drive a screw through the hole in the end of the tube and into the subfloor, then secure the tube with two clips (left).

2. Installing the thermostat sensor.

◆ With a utility knife, cut off the end of the thermostat tube about 6 inches from the plastic bushing.

◆ Feed the thermostat sensor into the tube (right) until it reaches the end of the tube fastened to the subfloor. (If the sensor does not slide easily, pull it back out and coat it with petroleum jelly.)

◆ Wrap electrical tape around the tube about 3 inches from the end to keep it from slipping through the bushing.

◆ Cut off the surplus sensor 3 inches or so beyond the end of the tube in the box.

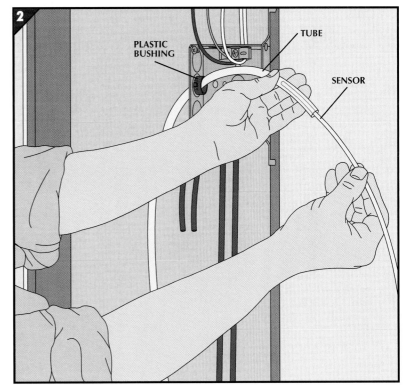

3. Testing the heating cable.

◆ Strip the ends of the wires of the heating cables and sensor *(page 121)*.

◆ To test the resistance in the circuit, touch one probe of a multitester to the red wire at one end of the heating cable and the other probe to the white wire at the other end *(right)*. The meter should give a reading lower than 150 ohms.

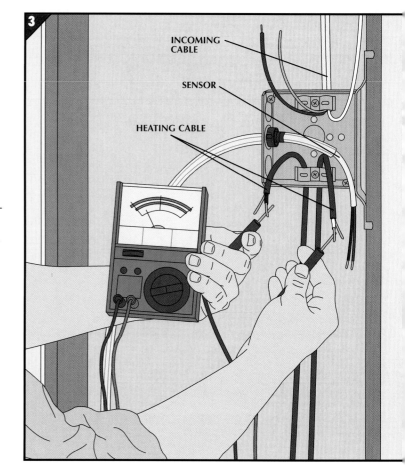

INCOMING CABLE

SENSOR

HEATING CABLE

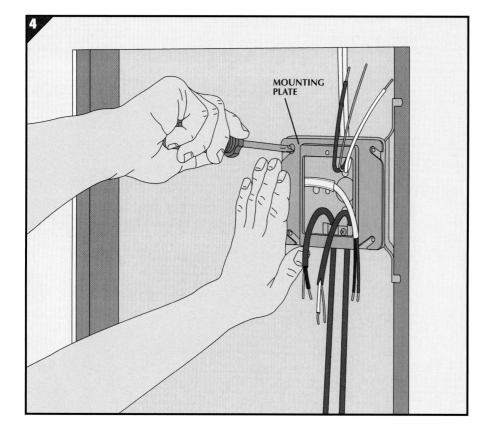

MOUNTING PLATE

4. Attaching the mounting plate.

◆ Place the mounting plate onto the electrical box and secure it with the screws provided *(left)*.

◆ Patch the open section of the wall with wallboard *(pages 63-65)*, cutting the patch to fit around the opening in the mounting plate.

5. Making the wire connections.

◆ Insert the insulated wires from the incoming cable, thermostat sensor, and heating cable into the thermostat terminals as indicated by the manufacturer and tighten each screw.

◆ With the wire cap provided, join the incoming-cable and heating-cable ground wires and two green jumper wires.

◆ Fasten one jumper wire to the ground screw on the electrical box, then insert the other one into the ground terminal on the thermostat and tighten the screw *(right)*.

For an installation with two heating cables, make the connections in the same way, but cap the pairs of red and white wires with the jumpers provided, then screw the jumpers to the terminals *(inset)*.

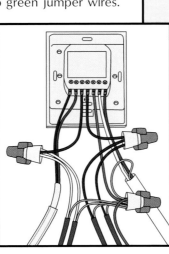

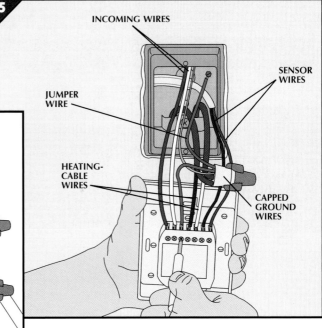

INCOMING WIRES

SENSOR WIRES

JUMPER WIRE

HEATING-CABLE WIRES

CAPPED GROUND WIRES

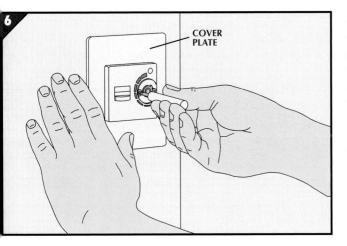

COVER PLATE

6. Securing the thermostat.

◆ Gently pry the control knob off the thermostat and loosen the screw for the cover plate.

◆ Insert the thermostat into the electrical box and screw it to the mounting plate.

◆ Position the cover plate on the thermostat and tighten the screw *(left)*, then replace the control knob.

◆ Have an electrician hook up the electrical cable to a GFCI-protected circuit breaker at the service panel.

◆ Follow the manufacturer's directions to set the thermostat.

ADDING THE MORTAR BED

Embedding the cables.

◆ Prepare a batch of premixed mortar.

◆ With the straight edge of a notched trowel, spread mortar onto the subfloor, applying a uniform bed that is thick enough to cover the heating cables completely *(right)*.

◆ Once the mortar bed has set, lay a new finish floor.

MORTAR

Appendix

Several of the projects in this book require basic wiring and plumbing skills. Illustrated on the following pages are techniques you will need to run new electrical cable and connect wiring to appliances or light fixtures; as well as methods for cutting and joining various types of water-supply pipes and drainpipe.

The techniques on these pages illustrate the basic methods you will need to run wiring for the projects in this book. First, however, familiarize yourself with local codes on residential wiring to determine what restrictions govern the work and whether some portions must be done by a licensed electrician. Before working on wiring at an existing fixture or switch *(pages 23-25 and 72)*, turn off the power to the circuit at the service panel *(below)* and test the circuit to be sure that the electricity is off *(page 120)*.

New Versus Existing Circuits: Electrical circuits in a typical home supply either 15 or 20 amps of power. When you are putting in wiring for a new appliance such as a steam bath or whirlpool, codes generally require that you run a dedicated circuit to the appliance from the service panel. If you simply tap into a nearby outlet or junction box to extend an existing circuit to the appliance, the additional electrical demands may exceed the allowed amperage and overload the circuit. If you are experienced in working with wiring systems and calculating electrical loads, however, you may be able to extend an existing circuit to an item such as a light fixture that uses very little power.

Check the requirements of the appliance manufacturer for the type of electrical cable to use; in general, No. 14 grounded cable is suitable for a 15-amp circuit, No. 12 for a 20-amp circuit. To estimate the amount of cable needed, measure the planned route and add 8 inches for each box, then add 20 percent to the total for unexpected deviations in the route.

Fishing Cable: Whenever possible, run cable through an unfinished basement or attic *(page 121)*, stapling it to joists or studs every $4\frac{1}{2}$ feet and within 12 inches of an electrical box. If necessary, you can fish cable through wall studs *(page 121)*.

 TOOLS

	Electric drill	Tin snips
	Fish tape	Electrician's
Screwdriver	Wallboard saw	multipurpose
Voltage tester	Cable ripper	tool

 **MATERIALS**

Electrical cable

Electrical tape
Wire caps

Turning off the power.
To shut off power to a circuit at the service panel, locate the breaker that controls the circuit and switch it to OFF *(above)*. For a fuse-type service panel, unscrew the fuse. If the circuits are not clearly labeled, shut off the power to all of them. Always double-check that the power is off before working on the circuit *(page 120)*.

> ⚠ **CAUTION**
>
> ## The Hazards of Aluminum Wiring
>
> *Between 1962 and 1972, nearly two million houses were wired with aluminum wiring. When connected to a dissimilar metal such as the copper-alloy terminals of a receptacle, the aluminum tends to corrode; and when the sheathing is removed, exposure to air causes the wire to oxidize. Both reactions increase the resistance in the wire, making it hotter when in use and therefore a fire hazard.*
>
> *Before you make any upgrades, check to see whether you have aluminum wiring: The sheathing is marked AL, and the wire itself is dull gray. Never attempt to repair or improve a system with aluminum wiring, except for replacing switches or fixtures. Exposed wire must be covered with a special antioxidizing paste; and all receptacles, switches, or other electrical devices must be the type marked CO/ALR. Any improvements must be in exact accordance with the National Electrical Code. Such work should be undertaken only by a licensed electrician.*

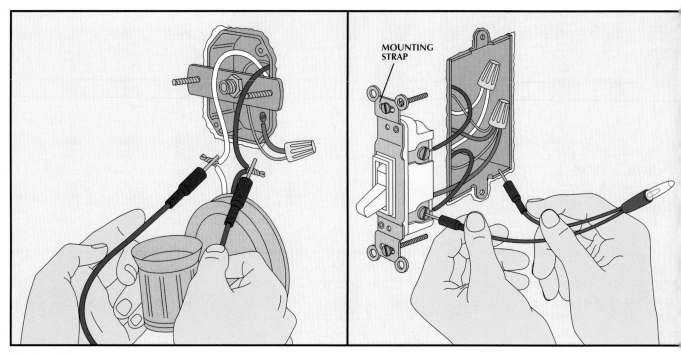

MOUNTING STRAP

Testing for power.

After turning off the circuit *(page 119)*, check that the electricity is off before working on an electrical box. For a light fixture, turn the wall switch off, then unscrew the base of the fixture and pull it away from the wall. Without touching the bare wire ends, carefully remove the wire caps. Turn on the wall switch, then touch one probe of a voltage tester to the ends of the black wires and the other probe to the box if it is metal, to the ground wire if the box is plastic.

Test between the black wires and white wires *(above, left)*, and between the white wires and the box or ground wire. If the tester lights in any of these cases, return to the service panel and turn off power to the correct circuit *(page 119)*.

For a wall switch, unscrew the cover plate and pull out the switch from the box by its mounting strap, then test between each brass terminal screw on the switch and the box if it is metal *(above, right)*, the ground wire if the box is plastic.

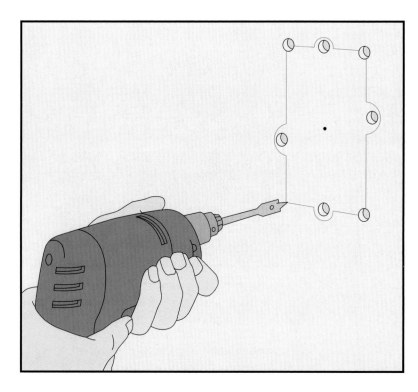

Making an opening for a box.

First, create a template: Place the electrical box face down on a sheet of thick paper and trace its outline, omitting the ears at the top and bottom *(page 122)*; then, mark an X within the outline. Place the template in the desired position with the X against the wall and trace its shape.

To cut the opening, turn off power to the circuits in the vicinity *(page 119)*. Then, drill a small hole in the center of the outline and check for obstructions with a bent coat hanger. With a $\frac{3}{8}$-inch bit, drill holes around the box outline as shown at left. Cut along the outline with a wallboard saw, being careful not to puncture the other side of the wall.

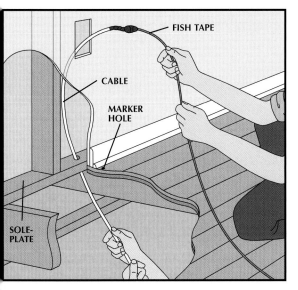

Fishing cable between floors.

To bring cable up from the basement, first drill a $\frac{1}{8}$-inch marker hole in the floor directly below the box opening. From below, drill a $\frac{3}{4}$-inch hole with a spade bit up through the soleplate in line with the marker hole. Feed a fish tape into the box opening and down behind the wall, and have a helper feed another tape up through the hole in the soleplate. Engage the tapes, then pull them down into the basement and disengage them. Strip a few inches of sheathing off the cable *(below)*, pass the wires through the hook of the upper tape, fold them back, and secure them with electrical tape. As your helper feeds cable up from below, pull the tape from above *(above)*.

Running cable through walls.

To fish cable behind a wall, locate the studs and cut holes 6 inches wide and 3 inches high at each location, then drill a $\frac{3}{4}$-inch hole through the center of each stud. Feed a fish tape through the hole in the stud next to the first opening, hook the other tape, and pull them out of the opening *(above)*. Disengage the tapes, attach the cable to the first tape, and pull it back through the stud. Fish the cable through the other studs in the same way.

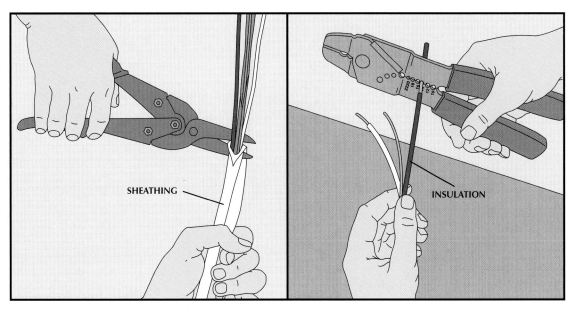

Preparing wires.

To make wire connections, the bare ends must be exposed. First, make a 6-inch slit in the outer sheathing of the cable with a cable ripper. Take care not to damage the insulation of the wires inside—even a small nick can cause a short. Bend back the sheathing and cut it off with tin snips *(above, left)*; trim off any paper liner. To strip the insulation off the wires, match the gauge of the cable you are using to the corresponding hole in a multipurpose tool. Close the tool over the wire $\frac{1}{2}$ inch from the end and rotate it a quarter-turn in each direction. Then, pull off the insulation without opening the tool *(above, right)*.

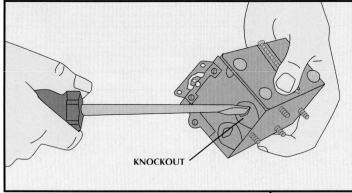

KNOCKOUT

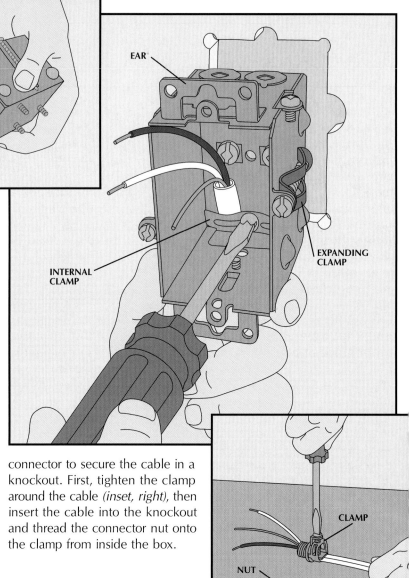

EAR

INTERNAL CLAMP

EXPANDING CLAMP

Installing a box.

Rectangular boxes for switches and outlets can be installed directly into wallboard. Octagonal boxes that will support the weight of a fixture must be attached to studs or joists.

To install a rectangular metal box like the one shown, first pry out one of the knockouts with a screwdriver *(inset, above)*, twisting it, if necessary, with pliers. Pass the cable through the knockout and under the clamp so about an inch of sheathing is exposed, then secure the clamp *(right)*. Insert the box in the opening and tighten the screws on the sides to draw the expanding clamps against the wallboard. A rectangular plastic box has an internal clamp that tightens automatically around the cable. To install this type of box, insert it in the opening and drive in the corner screws.

Octagonal boxes and some fixtures that have built-in junction boxes require a two-part connector to secure the cable in a knockout. First, tighten the clamp around the cable *(inset, right)*, then insert the cable into the knockout and thread the connector nut onto the clamp from inside the box.

CLAMP

NUT

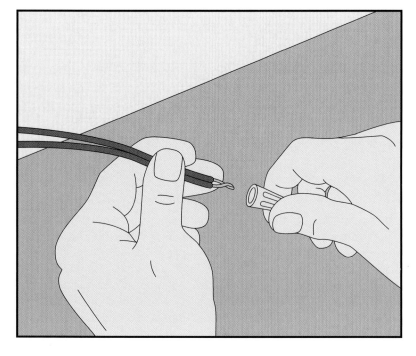

Joining wires with wire caps.

Place the wires to be connected side by side and twist the exposed metal ends together clockwise with lineman's pliers, then slide a wire cap onto the wires *(left)*. The cap must completely cover the bare wires—if any metal is visible, remove the cap and trim the ends of the wires without untwisting them. Push the wires firmly into the base of the cap and twist the cap clockwise until the connection is tight.

Plumbing Basics

The plumbing system of any home is made up of two networks of pipe—supply pipe that brings fresh water to fixtures, and drainpipe that carries away waste. Extending or rerouting these lines requires a few special tools and skills, as well as fittings in a variety of shapes, sizes, and materials *(below)*. Consult local codes before undertaking any plumbing project for requirements on pipe sizes, materials, and connections.

Supply Lines: Modern houses usually have supply pipes made of copper or a type of plastic called chlorinated poly-vinylchloride (CPVC). You can extend these lines with the same material, soldering on new copper pipes *(page 125)* or gluing on CPVC *(page 125)*. Or, you can add pipe of a different material, joining it to the existing with fittings made for the purpose.

Older homes may have threaded galvanized-steel pipe, which is joined with threaded fittings. You can extend this type with plastic pipe by screwing a plastic adapter to a steel fitting; for a steel-to-copper connection, use a special adapter called a dialetric union that prevents corrosion between the dissimilar metals.

Drainpipe: The fixture drainpipes in most modern homes are made of polyvinylchloride (PVC), a material that is glued together with PVC cement using the same methods as for CPVC.

In older homes, the fixture drainpipes are often made of galvanized steel. When you are installing a new plumbing fixture such as a sink or bathtub, simply unscrew the steel drainpipe from the nearest fitting and add a threaded PVC adapter onto the end of the run, then extend the line from the adapter with PVC pipe and fittings.

 TOOLS

Tube cutter or hacksaw

File
Knife
Wire fitting brush
Flux brush

Propane torch
Flameproof pad

 **MATERIALS**

Plumber's abrasive sandcloth

Paste flux
Solder
PVC or CPVC primer
PVC or CPVC cement

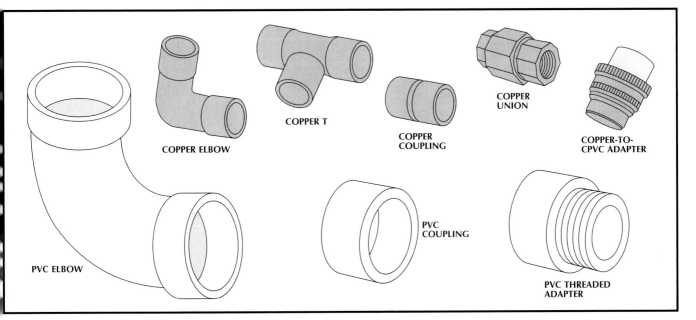

COPPER ELBOW

COPPER T

COPPER COUPLING

COPPER UNION

COPPER-TO-CPVC ADAPTER

PVC ELBOW

PVC COUPLING

PVC THREADED ADAPTER

A sampling of plumbing fittings.

The miscellaneous fittings for supply pipe and drainpipe vary in size and material, but they are similar in function. Whether you are working with plastic or copper, changes in the direction of pipe runs are made with elbows, which typically come in 45- and 90-degree turns.

Straight lengths of pipe are joined with couplings. With a fitting called a T, you can add a branch line to a straight run. Threaded supply-pipe unions can be unscrewed to disconnect the joint.

To change from one pipe material to another, you can use one of several types of adapters. Copper-to-CPVC adapters are soldered to copper pipe at one end and glued to CPVC pipe at the other. For mating plastic to galvanized steel, choose a plastic threaded adapter that can be screwed into the threads of a steel fitting. Use a dialetric union to join copper to steel.

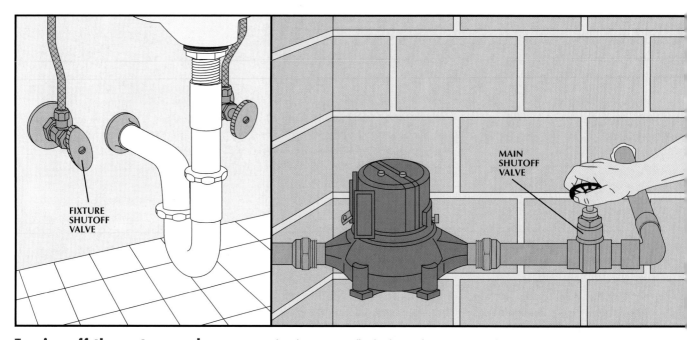

Turning off the water supply.

Sinks, toilets, and some other fixtures have shutoff valves that allow you to cut the water flow to that fixture alone *(above, left)*. Turn the shutoff valves fully clockwise, then open the faucets or flush the toilet to drain the pipes. If the fixture has no shutoff valves or the pipe must be cut on the supply side of the valve, close the main shutoff valve *(above, right)*—generally located near the water meter or where the supply pipe enters the house. Turn the shutoff valve fully clockwise, then drain the system by opening all the faucets in the house, starting at the highest point.

Cutting pipe.

The best way to cut a copper or plastic pipe is with a tube cutter intended for that material. Slide the cutter onto the pipe and turn the knob until the cutting wheel just bites into the pipe *(right)*. Rotate the cutter once around the pipe, retighten the knob, and turn the tool. Repeat the procedure until the pipe is severed. With the cutter's triangular blade, ream out the burrs inside the cut pipes. For galvanized-steel pipe, or to cut copper or plastic pipe in a confined area, a mini-hacksaw works well.

Remove ridges on the outside ends of cut copper pipe with a file; for plastic pipe, bevel the cut ends with a knife *(inset)*.

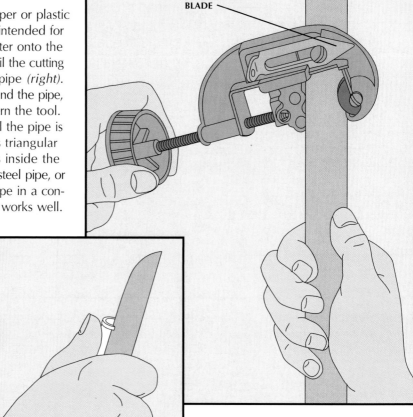

Joining copper.

With plumber's abrasive sandcloth, polish the cut ends of pipe to a distance slightly greater than the depth of the fittings you will be using to connect them. Then, with a wire fitting brush (inset), scour the inner surface of the fitting sockets. Once the pipe and fittings have been prepared, do not touch them—even a fingerprint could weaken the joint.

Brush a light coat of paste flux over the cleaned surfaces and place a fitting over one length of pipe, twisting it a quarter-turn. Protect the surface behind the joint with a flameproof pad, then play the flame of a propane torch over the pipe and fitting, keeping the tip of the flame about $\frac{1}{2}$ inch away. Touch a piece of solder to the fitting; if it does not melt on contact, heat the pipe and fitting a little longer. Hold the solder against the joint as shown at right until a bead of metal completely seals the rim.

 CAUTION   *Wear goggles and work gloves when using a propane torch.*

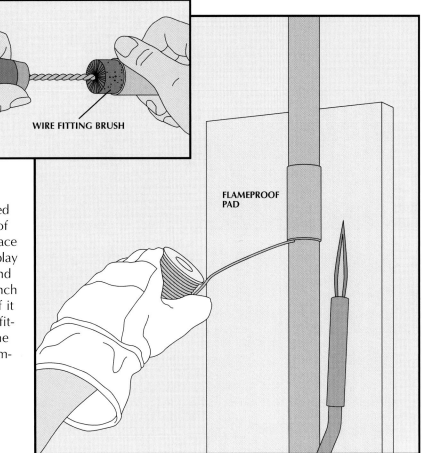

WIRE FITTING BRUSH

FLAMEPROOF PAD

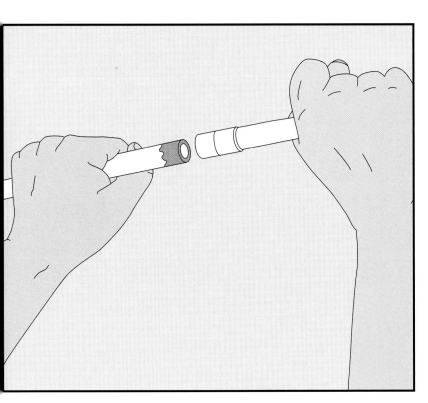

Joining plastic.

CPVC and PVC pipes are joined in the same manner, but each type of plastic requires its own primer and solvent cement. Brush the appropriate primer onto the end of a length of pipe and into the socket of a coupling. Apply a liberal coat of cement to the surfaces, then push the pieces together (left), giving them a quarter-turn, and hold them together for about 10 seconds. Wipe off excess cement with a clean, dry cloth. Do not run water through the pipe until the joint has cured for the time specified by the cement manufacturer.

When assembling straight runs of pipe with elbows or Ts, test-fit the entire assembly and draw pencil marks across each joint. After you have applied the primer and cement, push the parts together with the marks out of line, then turn them until the marks align.

INDEX

TIME® LIFE BOOKS

Time-Life Books is a division of Time Life Inc.

TIME LIFE INC.
PRESIDENT and CEO: Jim Nelson

TIME-LIFE BOOKS
PUBLISHER/MANAGING EDITOR:
  Neil Kagan
SENIOR VICE PRESIDENT, MARKETING:
  Joseph A. Kuna
VICE PRESIDENT, NEW PRODUCT
DEVELOPMENT: Amy Golden

HOME REPAIR AND IMPROVEMENT:
Bathroom Makeovers
EDITOR: Lee Hassig
DIRECTOR OF MARKETING:
  Wells P. Spence
Design Director: Kate McConnell
Text Editor: Karen Sweet
Editorial Assistant: Patricia D. Whiteford

Executive Vice President, Operations:
  Ralph Cuomo
Senior Vice President and CFO:
  Claudia Goldberg
Senior Vice President, Law & Business
  Affairs: Randolph H. Elkins

Vice President, Financial Planning &
  Analysis: Christopher Hearing
Vice President, Book Production:
  Patricia Pascale
Vice President, Imaging: Marjann Caldwell
Director, Publishing Technology:
  Betsi McGrath
Director, Editorial Administration:
  Barbara Levitt
Director, Photography and Research:
  John Conrad Weiser
Director, Quality Assurance: James King
Manager, Technical Services: Anne Topp
Senior Production Manager: Ken Sabol
Manager, Copyedit/Page Makeup:
  Debby Tait
Chief Librarian: Louise D. Forstall

ST. REMY MULTIMEDIA INC.
President: Pierre Léveillé
Vice President, Finance: Natalie Watanabe
Managing Editor: Carolyn Jackson
Managing Art Director: Diane Denoncourt
Production Manager: Michelle Turbide

Staff for *Bathroom Makeovers*

Series Editors: Marc Cassini, Heather Mills
Art Directors: Solange Laberge,
  Robert Paquet
Senior Editor: Brian Parsons
Editor: Rebecca Smollett
Assistant Editors: Stacey Berman,
  Jim Hynes, Robert Labelle
Designers: Jean-Guy Doiron, Robert Labelle
Photographers: Martin Girard,
  Maryo Proulx
Editorial Assistants: James Piecowye,
  Emma Roberts
Coordinator: Dominique Gagné
Indexer: Linda Cardella Cournoyer
Systems Director: Edward Renaud
Technical Support: Jean Sirois
Other Staff: Lorraine Doré,
  Francine Lemieux

PICTURE CREDITS

Cover: Photograph, Robert Chartier;
Art, Robert Paquet

Illustrators: La Bande Créative, Gilles Beauchemin, George Bell, Frederic F. Bigio from B-C Graphics, Jacques Perrault

The following illustration is based on material from: **29:** American Standard Inc.

Photographers: **End papers:** Robert Chartier. **8:** Kohler Co. **9:** Kohler Co. **10 (top):** Village. **10 (bottom):** American Standard Inc. **11:** Kohler Co. **13:** Maryo Proulx. **17:** Robert Chartier. **22:** Maryo Proulx. **31:** Robert Chartier. **33:** Maryo Proulx. **94:** Robert Chartier. **99, 101, 111:** Maryo Proulx. **38:** Jessie Walker. **39:** Ted Yarwood. **40 (top):** Rubbermaid Home Products, Inc. **40 (bottom):** Crandall and Crandall. **41:** Jean-Claude Hurni. **68:** Pittsburgh Corning Glass Block. **69:** Crandall and Crandall. **70 (top):** Jean-Claude Hurni. **70 (bottom):** FIAT Products Limited. **71:** Jean-Claude Hurni. **109:** Amerec Products.

ACKNOWLEDGMENTS
The editors wish to thank the following individuals and institutions: Amerec Products, Bellevue, WA; American Standard Inc., Morristown, NJ; American Standard Canada Inc., Toronto, Ont.; The Design Consortium San Diego, CA; Eagle Electric Manufacturing Co., Inc., Long Island City, NY; Jon Eakes, Montreal, Que.; Easy Heat Inc., New Carlisle, IN; FIAT Products Ltd., Winnipeg Man.; Louis V. Genuario, Genuario Construction Company, Inc., Alexandria, VA; Kohler Co., Kohler, WI; Leviton, Little Neck, NY; Maax, Inc., Sainte-Marie-de-Beauce, Que.; Pittsburgh Corning Corporation, Pittsburgh, PA; Reese, Tomases & Ellick, Inc., Wilmington, DE; Rubbermaid Home Products, Inc., Wooster, MA; F. Schumacher & Co., FSC Wallcoverings, New York, NY; Ira Shapiro, Architect, Redding, CT; Spartan of Canada, Lachine, Que.; Sussman Lifestyle Group, Long Island City, NY; Vermont American, Lincolnton, NC; World Floor Covering Association, Anaheim, CA.

**Library of Congress
Cataloging-in-Publication Data**
Bathroom makeovers / by the editors of
  Time-Life Books.
  p. cm. — (Home repair and improvement)
Includes index.
ISBN 0-7835-3924-X
1. Bathrooms—Remodeling—Amateur's
  manuals.
I. Time-Life Books. II. Series.
TH4816.3.B37B374   1998
643'.5—dc21   98-26904
                                    CIP

R 10 9 8 7 6 5 4 3 2 1